Reckless
YES

Reckless YES

EXCHANGING WORLDLY EASE
FOR GOD'S ETERNAL ADVENTURE

JOHNNA HENSLEY
FOREWORD BY AARON WATSON

REDEMPTION
PRESS

Published by Redemption Press, PO Box 427, Enumclaw, WA 98022. Toll-Free (844) 2REDEEM (273-3336).

Redemption Press is honored to present this title in partnership with the author. The views expressed or implied in this work are those of the author. Redemption Press provides our imprint seal representing design excellence, creative content, and high quality production.

Softcover: 978-1-951350-07-9
ePub: 978-1-951350-08-6
Audiobook: 978-1-951350-16-1
Library of Congress Catalog Card Number: 2023905273

Endorsements

Reckless Yes reminds us that even in life's most challenging moments, God remains faithful and we can trust Him to take us on the adventure of a lifetime.

> —**Bob Goff,** *New York Times* best-selling
> author of *Love Does, Dream Big,*
> *Everybody Always,* and *Undistracted*

In *Reckless Yes*, Johnna brilliantly weaves together biblical examples with a recounting of her own life. Her masterful storytelling serves as a gentle reminder of the beauty that unfolds, through even the darkest of days, when we boldly acquiesce to a life lived at the feet of Jesus.

> —**Erin Cuccio,** author of *Unraveled*
> and host of *Room for Lovely* podcast

TO HPVIP

This one's for you.
You changed my life and the entire world in big ways.
You taught me courage, and you showed me how to live life
without concern for what others think.

Your life encourages me to scream
"YES!" when God asks.
I love you.

Contents

Foreword

I met my friend Johnna in 2016 when her nine-year-old son, Hayden, emailed my tour manager asking for VIP backstage passes to watch my band and me soundcheck before one of my shows. I remember Hayden coming through the door with his wheelchair, trach tube, oxygen tank, feeding pump, and a smile bigger than Texas. The kid was a hoot, a handful, hilarious, and absolutely out of control! He was incredibly nosy and into everything. While he rambunctiously steered his wheelchair all over the place, his mom chased behind him, paranoid that he might knock over one of my guitars. I remember thinking, *Being that boy's mama looks exhausting!*

After we played a few songs for Hayden, we visited for a while, and he told me about his life, his family, and his two younger brothers. I came to realize that he loved country music even more than I did! He went on and on, asking more questions than any reporter I've ever worked with. At times, I felt like I was being interrogated! That kid had zero filter, and at the end of our talk he demanded my phone number so that he and I could continue our talks down the road. That little stinker and I hit it off like two peas in a pod.

My friendship with Hayden and his family continued over the next few years, and I was able to encourage Hayden during hospital stays and with FaceTime calls on his birthday. We even had a game night where he beat me in Uno and rubbed that in my face for months!

Watching Hayden grow up and overcome challenges has been an absolute blessing to me. He even inspired me to write a song called "To Be the Moon."

When I found out that the Hensley family was going to add foster care to their already busy equation, I was shocked and felt a bit of a panic attack. I was already blown away at how much Johnna had on her plate, and now she was going to open her home to more children? From the outside looking in, you could say she must be out of her mind. But it's a matter of the heart—a servant's heart, to be exact.

Johnna's story is inspiring, and I'm excited and honored that she asked me to write the foreword for her debut book, *Reckless Yes*. In it, Johnna is open about her imperfections and struggles, and she does not hold back when it comes to sharing her faith. She proudly confesses that without the guidance and love of Jesus, she wouldn't have the strength to push through the tough times while continuing to challenge herself to do more of what God asks of her. I love that she takes her personal situations and cross-references stories in the Bible, making each chapter of her book a Bible lesson within itself. Seeing the way she uses God's Word as her daily map has been so encouraging for me.

In this book you will enjoy watching how God moved in the life of one woman and changed her from the inside out. It will challenge and encourage you to take that leap of faith and allow God to do the same thing in your heart. Johnna's book is a reminder that life is full of struggles and difficulties, but we are not to let these earthly trials discourage us from treasures in heaven.

And with that, I now step off the stage and hand the mic over to the star of the show, Mrs. Johnna Hensley!

—*Aaron Watson*

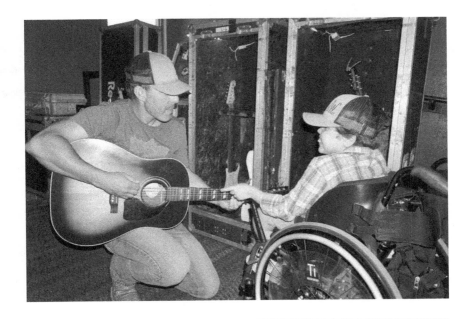

Aaron Watson and Hayden's first meeting in Denton, Texas, November 2016

Author's Note

When it came time to narrow down the title of this book, I struggled to select only one theme because there is so much I want to share with you. I've often found that the toughest lessons learned in life are easier to bear if they can encourage and help someone else. Trials help refine us. It's on the other side of refinement where we often discover our truest selves. It's from this place that I want to remind you of the importance of keeping an eternal perspective and not forgetting about the hope that awaits us in heaven. Let me encourage you to be brave and say yes to God's calling on your life. I challenge you to boldly choose the narrow path, even when the world offers you a wide, carefree, easy path. You'll find pieces of all of those lessons within this work. Much of what you'll read here, tucked away in the pages of my story, are moments when I chose to say yes to God's call for an adventurous life—a life that, to the naked eye, looks reckless.

When God presented me the challenging opportunity and adventure to share my story, I was privileged to respond with a yes. Because this project made its way into your hands today, I know God is real, and He has a plan. If this book came with a soundtrack, it would be one of twin toddlers crying, pulse oximeters beeping, tweens fighting, doorbells ringing, laundry tumbling, and, to be truthful, a lot of yelling, though in love. I wrote this book in the middle of total chaos . . . a.k.a. life. But the chaos of a house full of six kids of varying needs and ages has nothing on a God with a history of choosing the unqualified and equipping them to serve as His instruments to fulfill His purposes.

Completing this book was a tedious process of stealing away any treasured quiet moments I could find. It was waking up at 5:00 a.m. while the house was quiet, sitting alone at booth forty-four at my local Chick-fil-A restaurant after my morning school drop-off route, and renting library study rooms at odd hours of the day when I happened to find myself without children underfoot. In those sacred moments and spaces, I interpreted stacks of scribbled-on Post-it notes, flipped back through tear-stained journal pages, deciphered thought fragments typed as notepad entries on my iPhone, and pilfered through seven years of blog posts to create the book I now share with you. No matter the medium, the message was the same: *life is hard.* But you already know that. You're a living, breathing human, and that alone unites us in our struggle to tackle this broken world.

This is a story about meeting God at a fork in the road of my life. It's about who He is and how He proved Himself to me—how truly knowing Him changed the trajectory of my life. Allowing Him to lead has changed how I operate and respond to His calling on my life. I share these experiences with you because I want you to truly believe there is beauty in the brokenness we often face. I want you to trust God fully with your life and be willing to scream a reckless *Yes!* when He offers you an adventure.

The Bible tells us in Matthew 7:14 that "the gate is narrow and the way is hard that leads to life, and those who find it are few." When He calls you away from the wide, worldly path—the path of ease and self-focus, with no regard for God's sovereign guidance over your life—may you be one of the few who will courageously run toward the narrow path. Because it is there, on that difficult way, that you will find God and the adventurous life He calls you to.

Introduction

I'm not a fan of roller coasters. They've just never been my thing. I don't seek the adrenaline rush of hanging upside down and twisting through the air in a metal rocket. But my husband, Ryan, loves them, incidentally. When we were newly married, he and I took a trip to Six Flags over Texas in Dallas. To be a good sport, I pretended to be excited about this adventure and put on the bravest face I could, as any good newlywed would.

As we stood in a very long line to ride the famous Texas Giant, the flagship ride for the Six Flags franchise which I had never ridden before, I thought this would be the day I would tackle all my fears. We waited for what felt like half the morning until it was finally our turn to climb aboard the next vacant car. I walked right up to my seat, had a moment of clarity and overwhelming fear, and walked right out on the other side of the car. I ran, yelling behind me to Ryan that I'd meet him at the exit. I chickened out. I just couldn't do it. And I'm still lovingly mocked to this day for my wimpy amusement park companionship.

I lived the first two decades of my life that way. I'd try hard to put on my bravest face and psych myself up, but when the time came, I'd choose to run fast and hard away from anything new or scary. "Safety first" was my trusty motto. Taking the safe, conservative option came easy to me and kept me securely in the driver's seat of my own destiny.

I've been dealt countless moments in which I longed to escape the wild ups and downs this amazing flagship ride of life has to offer, which brave risk-takers seem to love as they soak up all the adrenaline that pumps through their veins.

I've often found myself running from a challenge and taking the easy way out when faced with various forks in the road. The appeal of the wide, easy path has always tempted me, but the wide, easy path wasn't the one I was being qualified for. I was chosen for the narrow path, however difficult it may be. It was on the challenging narrow path where I truly encountered and communed with the God I had only known about in theory. Years and years of hard, painful lessons have shaped me into the woman of God reflected in these chapters.

Circumstances placed me at a pivotal moment that I never saw coming, and it wasn't until I solidified my hope in heaven that I was able to eagerly choose the narrow path offered to me. This chance for an adventure would change everything about me—the way I make decisions, the way I view life, the way I handle adversity. For once, I decided to bravely trust God and go all in. I wanted to know what it would feel like to say yes. What if I just sat down, buckled up, and threw my arms in the air? What if I trusted the Operator and the adventure He was taking me on? The ultimate YOLO experience—to truly trust that in this brief, momentary life on earth, I'll only live once. What did I have to lose? And so, I said yes and leaned into the thrill. The ride hasn't slowed down yet, and now I see what all the adrenaline junkies were right about. There's nothing like this feeling in the world!

We all have choices we make in life—times when we hit a fork in the road and have to decide which path we'll take. I'd bet there have been times when you've wanted to enjoy the easy path, too, rather than tackle the challenge of the narrow path. I get it! Life as we know it is hard, even feeling unbearable at times. And though it can be challenging, there is also incredible hope and beauty to be discovered in it. Though my earthly life has had its share of hardships, I eagerly anticipate an eternal life that will restore each difficulty I have faced.

This book incorporates real-life stories from a special-needs mother, a foster mother, an adoptive mother of biracial children, and a homeschooling mother. I am all of those things—but I'm more. I am a daughter of the one true King, Jesus. When I thought each season and challenge I faced would surely break me, He was always there—even on the days when I didn't believe it. He saw me. He knew me. He loved me. He gave me hope incomparable. And, friend, He sees you, knows you, loves you, and offers you hope as well. It is because of what Jesus has done for us that I can say with certainty, to everyone standing at their own fork in the road, "It is worth it! He is worth it!"

I've structured this book to both tell my story and illuminate God's part in it, since He is actually the main character in my own story. Without the role He has played in my life, I would have no journey to share with you.

The odd-numbered chapters of this book will introduce a Bible character and reveal God's presence and plan in the life of that person, reminding us that God calls us to brave adventures and can be trusted in His sovereignty. We'll see that God is steadfast and steady for His people throughout all time and eternity. We'll witness His worthiness, holiness, and faithfulness, remembering along the way that the ups and downs of life for God's children have a different meaning than for those who have yet to trust in Jesus. Let me encourage you to read with an open mind and remain curious about what God may be trying to speak to your heart.

In the even-numbered chapters, I share personal stories that tell the progression of my life, beginning with my childhood and ending in present day. These chapters tie into the biblical teaching about God's character and coincide with how He was moving in my life at the time. You can consider the chapters as complementary pairs; there are seven sets of chapters that convey various seasons of my life and biblical teachings.

The message of all the chapters is to remind us that when we truly trust God and believe He is who He says He is, we can live our lives in complete surrender to His plan and goodness. I hope you will begin to notice God moving in mighty ways in your own story for His glory.

Let me encourage you, when you come to a fork in the road of your life, don't deliberate so long that the only path left is the wide one that leads to destruction. Choose to go all in with the risky, reckless, narrow path and see what beauty there is to discover on the road less traveled. Let's not waste our lives waiting in line for a roller coaster we're too scared to try. Jump right on—heck, get in the front car, buckle up, and throw those hands in the air! Because the thing about this ride called life is that it only runs once. There are no do-overs. We cannot waste our one ride wondering what all the other people in the line will think of us. We cannot spend all our days in careful contemplation, never taking a step forward, or worse yet, running away from an adventure.

My prayer is that this book will challenge you to bravely choose to meet Jesus on the narrow path that leads to life. This is my manifesto to you, dear reader. Be brave, choose the challenge, and enjoy the beautiful adventure God offers. Don't waste this ride, this adventure, this journey, because life is but a vapor. Go all in with God and be reckless.

CHAPTER ONE

Defining the Relationship (D. T. R.)

Through him we have also obtained access by faith
into this grace in which we stand, and we rejoice
in hope of the glory of God.

ROMANS 5:2

I've been walking with God for thirty years, give or take. For some of those years, I was stuck to Him like glue, holding on for dear life. But for much of that time, He and I were in the same vicinity, yet I often wandered off with Him barely in my sight. I was just close enough to say I was "with Him," but I wasn't earnestly seeking after Him. Of course, He never moved; I was the one floating away from His steady presence.

Have you had the same experience? You know you need to stay close to your Shepherd, but your senses are distracted by life or by watching people who are seemingly having more fun than you, dancing carefree through life.

You may be familiar with the popular biblical story of the Israelites fleeing Egypt under the leadership of Moses. (Charlton Heston and *The Ten Commandments*, anyone?) God called Moses, miraculously, through a burning-bush encounter and equipped him to be the spokesperson for God's chosen people, the Hebrew nation. Moses, with help from his big brother, Aaron, demanded that Pharaoh let their people go. Ten unique plagues against the Egyptians later, Pharaoh finally relented.

Once freed from Egypt, the Israelites spent the next forty years wandering the desert, although they weren't lost. They were following God's leading. Through a cloud by day and a pillar of fire by night, He led, and they followed.

Flipping through the pages of Exodus, we see the frustrating sin pattern of the Israelites unfold and find ourselves wondering, *Why can't these people just act right?* But if I were a betting woman, I'd wager we would commit the same sins given the opportunity. Because we do. Every day. We make idols and place them above God. We fail to trust His plan. We daydream about the good old days and misperceived ease of previous circumstances of bondage. It's much easier to identify sin in a Bible story than to be aware of the sin we're currently walking in, isn't it?

One of the major sinful moments the Israelites participated in during their forty-year journey was the creation of the golden calf (Exodus 32). While Moses was up on the mountain for forty days speaking with God and receiving His laws, the people got antsy. They convinced Aaron to whip up a god they could worship while they waited for Moses to return. And Aaron obliged.

In His omnipresence, God knew what was going on at the bottom of the mountain, so He let Moses in on the breaking news. He told Moses, "Go down, for *your* people, whom *you* brought up out of the land of Egypt, have corrupted themselves" (Exodus 32:7, emphasis mine). Exodus 32:9–10 tells us that God was keenly aware this was a stiff-necked people, and He needed some alone time because His hot wrath was about to consume them.

The next verse tells us how Moses responded. He implored God to turn from His burning anger and relent from this disaster against the people. And you know what? The Lord heard Moses, and He relented. God and Moses were two parties actively involved in a relationship. They were in community with each other. They were close enough that Moses knew God's feelings and was confident enough in their relationship that he spoke freely with God and begged Him to change His mind.

God is relational. He interacts with His people. He is involved in the lives of those He has called. Sometimes we may not believe God could possibly be interested in our daily lives and struggles because we assume He doesn't want to hear from us. He's got the whole world in His hands, after all. Surely He's got bigger, more important things to contend with than our day-to-day trials and hurts.

Does this sound like you? Is something keeping you from drawing closer to God? If you're resting securely in your relationship with Him in this moment, that is such a beautiful, safe place to be. But it could be that your past mistakes and regrets have convinced you that God is ashamed of you and doesn't want to restore the rift between you. Or maybe you believe you've got to be perfect before you present yourself to Him, so you put off coming to the throne and being known by your Creator.

That's the space I lived in for many years of my life. I found it impossible to comprehend that God delighted in me as His daughter. Coming to this understanding was a process that took years and was achieved by studying the Bible, learning God's character, and investing in Christian counseling. Seeing the character of God as a loving Father in the Old Testament played a monumental role in my relationship with the Lord. I had grown up feeling unworthy and unnoticed, but the Bible offered me good news. It showed me there is a *Person* who is head over heels in love with me, adores me, and values everything I have to say. And He knows my name—the spelling and pronunciation, to boot!

He knows your name too, by the way, and He wants to see it in His book (Luke 10:20). He wants you to be with Him for eternity. But He also wants a relationship with you *now*, on this side of heaven.

If you've ever done a full Bible-reading plan, you may have stopped at Leviticus. A lot of people throw in the towel at that point because it's full of laws and rules and not much narrative story. But tucked away in the pages of Leviticus, we see a good, good Father who makes incredible provisions for the health, safety, and protection of His people.

Leviticus 19 shows us that God made a plan for the poor to have food. He said, "When you reap the harvest of your land, you shall not reap your field right up to its edge, neither shall you gather the gleanings after your harvest. And you shall not strip your vineyard bare, neither shall you gather the fallen grapes of your vineyard. You shall leave them for the poor and for the sojourner: I am the LORD your God" (Leviticus 19:9–10). He was Provider for the people, especially the poor and the sojourner. He made a way when there was no way, even back in Leviticus.

In the New Testament, we discover that God sent His own Son, Jesus, to earth to walk as a man. Jesus experienced the same things we do: grief, betrayal, sadness, exhaustion, hunger, and thirst. Yet unlike us, He was sinless in all circumstances. As such, He was the perfect sacrifice, qualified to pay the penalty for our sins. Through His death on the cross and His resurrection three days later, Jesus overcame death and made a way for us to overcome it as well. It was in God's provision as Father that He sent His Son to pave the way for you and me to be adopted into His family and offer us the chance to have a relationship with Him.

Because I have accepted this free gift of salvation, I have complete hope and healing in Jesus. As a daughter of the King, I now find my true identity in the family of God and nowhere else. I know what authentic, pure love feels like. And when you're loved like crazy by your Creator, you are free indeed.

I encourage you to not delay in coming to Jesus. If seeking reconciliation with God has been on your to-do list but has never made its way to the top, there is no time like the present to heed the Spirit's calling. If past mistakes and sins have kept you from coming to Him and accepting the free gift of salvation, there is no time like today to make things right.

Perhaps you've been hurt by the church. Or maybe you've experienced tremendous hardships and struggles, and it feels like

God has abandoned you. Or could it be that you know the Lord but aren't walking deeply in connection with Him? Maybe you don't know Him yet but you're intrigued by what salvation means and what a relationship with Him would be like. Perhaps you just aren't sure why you should love and trust Him.

We were all created in God's image. We were created for relationships with one another and most importantly, with Him. Any relationship involves two parties. He never changes, but we're prone to wander. No matter what you do for work, your worldly accomplishments, or who depends on you, if you are a follower of Christ, you must first solidify your relationship with the Lord. And from that place of security, you operate in your daily life.

This is a daily reminder for me. It is a constant battle between my flesh and my heart. The Enemy is great at convincing us that our children, spouse, work, or status should be our number-one priority. Those are all wonderful things. But our first priority has to be a real, interactive relationship with God. It is why we were created.

When we're in a relationship with someone, we know things about them, such as their likes and dislikes. We trust them, and we communicate with them frequently. The same is true when we're in an active relationship with our heavenly Father. As we constantly learn more about Him, our relationship grows and we deepen our trust and faith in Him.

Could it be that the reason we are miserable—running from here to there and back again, reviewing our Pinterest boards at stoplights to make sure we hit the mark for our kids' birthday party decor, scroll Instagram constantly to see how we measure up against our favorite influencers, sync our Fitbit regularly so we can show the world we dominated the *Workweek Hustle* challenge—is that we have our priorities mixed up? Those things are not what life is about! They never will be. Some of the distractions in our lives may be lovely, but when our time on earth concludes, none of them will hold any value.

Jesus is both historical and present. We couldn't write prayers in a journal to Abraham Lincoln, a historical figure, and expect Honest Abe to reveal himself to us throughout our day. But Jesus, who was historical, is also alive and present today, working in the hearts of His followers in real time. If you have accepted Christ as Savior, the Bible says you have received the Holy Spirit, one of the three persons of the Trinity. The Spirit directs believers in their heart posture, decision-making, and walk with the Lord every day.

Though the Spirit indwells me, I still have moments of feeling isolated and discouraged. Even when my heart may break or life's circumstances feel unbearable, I am not alone. When my pride wants me to hide my tears and my sorrow from Him, my Father is with me in my hurting. Scripture tells us, "You keep track of all my sorrows. You have collected all my tears in your bottle. You have recorded each one in your book" (Psalm 56:8 NLT). That sounds like a good, good Father who is keenly interested in His daughter.

I wonder if one of the reasons He writes our hurts in a book is that eventually, when we see Him in glory, all will be restored. He is keeping the record so He can set it right. I trust that whatever we endure on this earth is for a greater purpose that we cannot fathom this side of heaven. No matter how miserable the sufferings are, there's a greater good, and we can rest in that.

∽

After the golden calf incident, Moses headed down the mountain, and his anger burned against his people and his brother, Aaron. The Israelites' sin had significant consequences. Since the payment for sin is death (Romans 6:23), three thousand Israelites were killed that day due to their rebellion.

God agreed to send the Israelites into the promised land; however, He would not go with them. After hearing this offer, Moses told God, "If you won't go with us, don't bother; I won't go if you don't come too" (Exodus 33:15, paraphrase mine). God agreed that He would "do this thing that you have spoken; for you have found grace in My sight, and I know you by name" (Exodus 33:17 NKJV). Incredible! Can you imagine hearing God tell you directly that He knows you by name? This is what the Word of God tells us! "Fear not, for I have redeemed you; I have called you by name, you are mine" (Isaiah 43:1).

After hearing the news that His presence would accompany the Israelites all the way to the promised land, Moses had one more request for God. "Please show me your glory" (Exodus 33:18). In response to this request, God reminded Moses that no one could see His face and live. But God did offer consolation for Moses. He told him, "Here is a place by Me, and you shall stand on the rock. So it shall be, while My glory passes by, that I will put you in the cleft of the rock, and will cover you with My hand while I pass by. Then I will take away My hand, and you shall see My back; but My face shall not be seen" (Exodus 33:21–23 NKJV).

I've often had moments when I wanted to see God face-to-face, to be near Him and commune with Him. I want to be comforted by His presence in my sadness and pain. There are times in life when the only thing left for us to do is hit our knees and cry to our Father. Our Dad. In such times we may ask to see Him and His glory. Yet that's not an option for us this side of heaven.

Perhaps though, in times when we feel utterly alone, it is because there is only room for One when we are hidden in the cleft of the rock, and His hand covers us as His presence moves by.

May we all strive for a relationship with our Father like the one Moses had—when we truly understand that His presence is what we need, more than success or stuff or status.

Are there areas of your life you've turned into golden calves? Perhaps a shiny trinket, your next vacation or distraction from reality, or the pursuit of happiness rather than holiness? What will you do to prioritize your relationship with God? Are you willing to take the next step and inch closer to your Shepherd?

Moses wasn't willing to trade the world's most delicious milkshakes made from the land of milk and honey if it cost him the nearness of God, communing with Him, and being hidden by Him in the cleft of the rock. May the same be true of us.

CHAPTER TWO

Outlier

Outlier (n.)—a person or thing differing from all other members of a group or set[1]

I never have fit in. I've always been the square peg trying to fit in a round hole, feeling like I didn't belong anywhere. I like to joke that I was born a grown woman, strictly business and lacking the skills needed for imaginative play with peers. Pretending a toy or doll was alive when it clearly was not felt foolish and childish to me. The only pretend play I could get on board with were scenarios where I was in charge—like running a classroom with my younger brother as one of the many students on my fabricated roster or operating a cash register to run my made-up business—of which I was the boss, obviously. Always the protector, I played

"Mom" and attempted to shield my baby brother from any perceived harm, whether during our playtime or in reality.

In high school, while my fellow students were attending parties and having movie nights, I worked countless odd jobs at restaurants and clothing retailers, saving my money with hopes of attending college. After graduation, when most of my classmates flew to Mexico or Europe for their senior trips, I headed to "Harvard on the Highway," the popular nickname for the community college in the next town over, to earn affordable hours for the college basics. Some might say that is just a remarkable work ethic, but I know now I was chasing something. From the very beginning, I was chasing a different ending.

I'm a fourth-generation East Texan and proud of it. Life behind the pine curtain is special. I didn't realize what a gift it was to grow up in a forest until I left the quiet woods and ventured out into the world. And anywhere else in the world was what I was after. For most of my life, I lived in constant anticipation of a brighter day ahead—a way out—a path that was different from the one I started out on.

The home where I grew up was one of hustle and hard work. My parents taught me the value of a strong work ethic. Blue-collared, button-up shirts with first names embroidered on white patches, well-worn Red Wing work boots leaning in the corner of the living room floor, cafeteria hairnets of just the right shade of dark auburn—these images will forever be dear to my heart. In our house, my brother and I were shown true grit. For most of my life, both my mother and father had two to three jobs at a time, working their fingers to the bone to provide for us. Thankfully, the ends met most months, and we certainly understood the value of having a roof over our heads and food on the table. There was no doubt that my brother and I were taught what it meant to not give up when things got hard.

Though my family of origin shared a mailing address, there wasn't much else our family unit had in common. My father ate his meals separately from my brother, my mother, and me. He worshiped at a different church than we did. He spent his free time working side jobs or cultivating his garden rather than cultivating relationships with his family. When I became involved in extracurricular activities at school, like twirling and band, my father never once came to see me perform.

My mother, on the other hand, was present at every football game, concert, band contest, and majorette tryout I was a part of. She took me to private clarinet lessons and twirling camps on college campuses hours from our home, and she encouraged me to pursue my collegiate goals. Most people at my high school assumed my parents were divorced and that was why my dad was unavailable. Sometimes I went with that storyline because it flowed easier than admitting my dad was at home watching television alone.

And so I built tall, thick walls of protection all around me. If the walls were thick enough, and my teenage attitude sassy enough, maybe my parents wouldn't know how badly I was hurting. Then I could convince the world (and myself) that I was strong, tough, independent, and driven. The last thing I wanted anyone to know was that inside my tightly squeezed fists was pure, cynical, jaded hurt.

I believe the experiences we have and the obstacles we face as children shape us into the adults we become. Now, as a parent sitting on the other side of my childhood, it's with fresh eyes. I can appreciate that my parents were doing the best they could with what they had. Parents shoulder an incredibly heavy load in being responsible for their children's every physical and emotional need.

If you're a parent, you probably bear the burden of feeling like you're not doing enough for your children or not discipling them enough. You constantly wonder if you've prepared them for the real world.

I know my parents loved me and cared deeply about me. Their love and care presented differently than the "typical" American family, but my mom and dad certainly did, and still do, love me. I accept and honor all that they did for me. My childhood shaped me into a young woman with wonderful character traits but also significant wounds.

Maybe your childhood did the same to you. Or did adulthood wound you? Perhaps it was a marriage that failed. A wayward adult child. A business you built from the ground up that you watched crash and burn. I bet you've experienced some things in your life you wish had shaken out differently. A tweak here, a modification there—just think how much better life could have been. But here's the thing: the Bible tells us that "all things work together for good to those who love God" (Romans 8:28 NKJV). *All things.* What would happen if we accepted the difficult, challenging things in good faith that God can and will use them to work together for our good?

ᦐᦐᦐ

Even as a small child, I knew that if only I could go to college, I could change the trajectory of my life. My idol became the pursuit of a degree and a career with an ample paycheck—not for money or to collect treasures and trinkets but so I could create a way out of living paycheck to paycheck. I wanted to avoid constant fights, arguments, and battles over money . . . or the lack thereof. I chased after a way out of the cycle modeled to me of working just to survive.

In an effort to escape the noise and loud disagreements at home, I set out to pave a new path for myself. I thought becoming a first-generation college graduate would solve all my problems, because surely white-collared workers didn't have this hurt and unrest like blue-collared families did, right?

But money wasn't the solution I needed. The relief I sought could only come from God—although it would be years before that healing began.

The year before graduating high school, I realized that if I could secure a top 10 percent spot in my class, I would be guaranteed acceptance to any state college in Texas. With my eyes on the prize and a dream in my heart to attend Texas A&M University, I worked hard. The high school registrar and I became quite close with my weekly visits to her office to check the class rankings for the week. Thankfully, I reached my goal and was accepted into my first-choice college and two others. This was my chance to change my entire life. Days after graduation, I packed up boxes in my bedroom and made plans for the fall semester.

August rolled around, and I loaded down my decade-old hand-me-down car, a Geo Prizm, with all my belongings and headed for College Station, Texas, and I never looked back. Moving back home for summers was not an option for me. I had a goal to reach, and I put all my attention to it.

Rather than move into a dorm, I opted to rent an efficiency apartment by myself—a decision I now regret with the clarity hindsight has to offer. But at the time, the best thing I could do for myself was to live alone, make my own decisions, enjoy solitude in silence, and focus solely on work and school. And that's exactly what I did.

Before the first day of classes even commenced, I had a full semester of college hours completed and was utilizing that strong work ethic built into my DNA. I always had a job (or two), and I took summer classes to stay ahead.

There's no better motivation to complete school quickly than paying for it on your own dime. Sitting beside fifth-year seniors in the business school, I took eighteen hours of classes a semester and remained on track to wrap up college in three years.

Time flies when you're having fun (and working wild hours), and before I knew it, the final summer of college was upon me. I rushed from a new job orientation straight to the first day of a summer course called Marketing Research 323. Always running late and pressed for time, I wasn't fully prepared for the first day of class and arrived without a notepad or any notebook paper.

Although sometimes unprepared, I was always scrappy, so when the professor began reviewing the syllabus and plans for the semester, I pulled out the Texas Digital Systems handbook from the work orientation I had just come from. I fashioned the blank back of the workbook into my scratch paper. Reduce, reuse, recycle—perfect!

As I was frantically jotting notes, a classmate in my row peered into my highly protected, introverted space bubble. This tall, brown-haired stranger leaned over and whispered, "Where did you get that paper?" The nerve of this guy! I mean, it wasn't conventional, but I was being resourceful, and I couldn't believe he would dare ask me that.

I curtly answered, "From my *job*," and turned my attention to the professor mapping out the rest of the semester for us.

This stranger kindly informed me that he was curious because he had just attended orientation at that same company and began his new job there that week as well. What were the odds? We introduced ourselves and described where our offices were located in the building we would be sharing for work.

Then, as often happens in expedited summer courses, we were instructed to form groups to conduct a cooperative research project that would be the main portion of our class credit. Since my newfound coworker and I were already acquainted, we joined up with two other students, and our team was born. We spent the rest of the summer not only as coworkers but as group mates. I couldn't seem to outrun my new friend.

~∞~

It's an interesting irony to be raised in the church yet not truly know the closeness of Jesus. Along with being a fourth-generation Texan, I was a fourth-generation Southern Baptist. If the church doors were open, I was at church . . . Sunday morning, Sunday night, Wednesday evening, prayer meetings, tent revivals.

My father, though raised Southern Baptist, worshiped in Pentecostal and charismatic churches. My paternal grandmother, aunt, and uncle toured churches in deep East Texas, Louisiana, and across the South, singing Southern gospel music. My uncle, an incredible piano player who played only by ear, provided soulful music while my aunt and grandmother performed and led crowds in worship. Church and gospel music was the soundtrack of my childhood—Christmas cantatas and choir robes all part of the standard Southern church experience.

Yet there was a breakdown somewhere, a disconnect. The songs we sang about our old-time religion and the sermons we heard about the hell we needed to avoid fell short when it came to teaching me about the beautiful relationship I was invited into with God. These songs and sermons were mostly geared toward eternity, which is wonderful. We should keep our focus on eternity, absolutely! But in the context of my own childhood, I missed the message that God is available and eager for a relationship with me in the here and now, not just in heaven after my earthly life has ended. I did not fully comprehend that He has wonderful, good plans for me here on earth too.

I understood the gospel and accepted Jesus as my Savior at the age of eight, but I spent the majority of my Christian life disengaged from God. Living your formative years with a father who shows little interest in you can skew your perception of a doting heavenly Father. To actually believe that the Creator of the universe delighted in me and enjoyed me and was available to hear my thoughts, fears, and concerns? No way! I didn't buy it. I was thankful for the free gift of salvation, of course, but I completely missed the part about a relationship.

Because my earthly father had never been eager for a relationship with me, I didn't understand my loving heavenly Father. No matter how many Sunday school lessons I sat through, how many VBS songs I learned, or how many times I pledged to the Christian flag, I couldn't grasp that God longed to spend time with me. This disconnect affected me more than I fully understood in my childhood, teen years, and early twenties. I spent most of my life, as many do, focused on a works-based system of salvation, avoiding any major sins and staying as squeaky-clean as possible, in an effort to stay on God's "good side"—trying hard not to upset Him yet never enjoying the freedom He invited me to walk in.

Coming into adulthood, I began to see tiny glimpses of how God was ready to do a mighty work that would change me completely, if only I would trust Him. There were situations and relationships in my young-adult and college years that were not God's best for me. I felt a certain shift and a clear leading to trust God and to cut out the ways I was spending my time that weren't His design for me. Consequently, I found myself in some of the toughest, loneliest times I have ever been through, but those moments were necessary to prepare me for what was to come.

Sitting alone in my apartment, eating ramen noodles, studying on weekends when everyone else seemed to be out with friends, breaking things off with my high school and college boyfriend, whom

I had fully anticipated marrying—all these moments were baby steps I took toward God and His sovereignty. I was still uncertain about the direction He was taking me, but I trusted Him nonetheless.

I didn't realize then that God was about to heal my every wound, heartache, and hurt from the past in a most unusual way. I had no idea that healing the broken parts of me would require my world to be shattered to the core. I was not yet aware that all those songs and sermons were about to come to life in a very real, beautiful way. I just had to get out of my own way first.

In the winter of 2003, after what felt like an eternity of loneliness, the Lord brought into my life a wonderful group of friends. In February 2004, we attended a country concert at a historic venue in College Station, Texas. While there I ran into my handsome, dark-haired group mate named Ryan from marketing class. While he was waltzing me around the hardwood floor, he asked me out. I overlooked his lack of dancing skills and agreed to a first date.

We got engaged in August 2004, and five months later we were married. What a year that was! Our life together has continued in the same whirlwind fashion ever since.

When God orchestrated our marriage, I am certain the gates of hell shook a little bit that day. The Enemy surely knew God was getting ready to move mountains for the kingdom.

I've come to learn that it's in our broken pieces where we find the most beauty. On the other side of hurt, heartache, and pain, I am delighted to say that though I am scarred, I am also healed. I can forgive the people and circumstances that once wounded me because I have watched God use the ashes of pain to create extraordinary beauty.

Accepting that I am a child of Abba Father, and understanding who and how He is, has helped me extend grace to my earthly father. Knowing and believing that I am a daughter of the most engaged Father, I've been able to let go of the idol I made of having the "ideal" father. I am restored. God has filled in all the gaps and repaired wounds I kept hidden for decades. And though this path has been a rocky one, it has been fruitful.

God can make beauty from ashes and turn mourning into dancing—for you, for me, for all of us. He can rebuild and restore all things for His glory. Do you have parts of your story that have crushed you? Would some healing and restoration be a salve on open wounds you've yet to treat? Let's walk through healing together. God loves you and desires a relationship with you. And He is the only one who can offer true healing and hope.

Ryan and Johnna's wedding day in Longview, Texas, January 15, 2005

CHAPTER THREE

God's Orchestra

Not only that, but we rejoice in our sufferings.

ROMANS 5:3

If you are in search of a good read full of drama and suspense, a love story with romance, talking donkeys, and giants, may I suggest giving the Bible a chance as your next book club pick? All those stories and more are tucked away in the threads of Scripture, ready to unfold before your eyes, not merely as your next page-turner but to transform your life.

In Genesis, the first book of the Bible, you'll meet a character named Joseph. If you think your family is wild and dramatic, allow me to introduce you to Joseph and his eleven brothers. These twelve men all had the same father, Jacob; the same grandfather, Isaac; and the same great-grandfather, Abraham. God had called Abraham and made a covenant with him, promising to bless the whole earth through his offspring, the newly established line of Israelites (Genesis 12). Jacob's sons eventually represented the twelve tribes of Israel.

In his house full of twelve boys, Daddy Jacob's favorite is Joseph, hands down, every time. And everyone knows it—talk about sibling rivalry. And not just the "You're not invited to Christmas dinner this year" kind of drama. Think more along the lines of "Let's plot to murder our brother because Dad bought him better clothes than us." And some people think the Bible is boring!

Through a series of events, the brothers' plot to murder Joseph fails to come to fruition, so they sell him into slavery, and he is sent to Egypt (Genesis 37:27–28). While there, Joseph lands a gig working in the home of one of Pharaoh's high commanding officers, a man named Potiphar. Joseph becomes quite successful in his new role.

Four times in chapter 39 alone (verses 2, 3, 21, and 23), we are told explicitly that the Lord was with Joseph. One could begin to reason that *because* the Lord was with him and *because* Joseph exhibited God's character in his daily work activities as a slave, his success as a man and in his position was attributed to God's presence with him.

Sitting on this side of Genesis, it's easy for us to see how a series of unfortunate events was actually God orchestrating a miraculous plan to work great good for countless people. Of course, it's doubtful that Joseph had the same sentiment that fateful day on the bumpy wagon ride to Egypt, listening to the sound of his shackles clanking together, feeling the betrayal and pain from his brothers' scheme of trying to off him. In his moments of fear and sadness, he was alone and betrayed, most likely feeling forgotten by God. Yet God was still present and working, as we'll soon discover.

During my formative years, I had no idea how God was going to use the seasons of difficulties, diligence, and perseverance I had to walk through to affect my future. Oftentimes we can't anticipate how God will take something that feels like a mess and turn it around for good. When I was working and saving and enduring challenges as a teen and young adult, God was building into my character the traits I would need to endure even more hardships yet to come—and heal my soul through them. I only saw the struggles, but God, in His sovereignty, stood outside of time and was working to develop me into the woman He designed me to be.

Certainly we've all had moments where we feel alone and shackled, like a prisoner being dragged off to a destination against our will. Maybe it's a cross-country move or a career change you weren't anticipating. Or suddenly becoming a widow with a house full of children and a million pieces to pick up. It could simply be the endless drudgery of the daily mundane carpools, dinners, laundry, and chores. We've all been brought to places that were different from what we anticipated.

What do we do in those moments? How do we pick up the pieces of our unmet expectations and sadness to take the next step and move forward? Let's see what we can learn from Joseph.

Things certainly took a wild turn for Joseph. Genesis 39:7 tells us that Potiphar's wife took a liking to Joseph and found him quite handsome. She became quite persistent during her interactions with him on multiple occasions and made her intentions known. But Joseph was consistent in his attempts to honor God by not committing "this great wickedness and sin against God" (verse 9).

One day, Mrs. Potiphar grabbed Joseph by the sleeve and tried to seduce him again, but he did the honorable thing and fled, leaving his garment behind. Joseph's rejection did not go over well with Potiphar's wife. She responded by fabricating a lie, claiming Joseph had attacked *her*. His garment in her possession proved his "guilt." With no more favor to be found in his master's sight, it was off to prison Joseph went. Yet the Lord was *still* with Joseph—even within the prison walls. And He was still working in Joseph's life.

After settling into his new environment, Joseph continued to have God's favor upon him. In no time, he became a person of honor and authority in the prison because "the LORD was with him; he showed him kindness and granted him favor in the eyes of the prison warden" (Genesis 39:21 NIV). Behind those prison walls, Joseph showcased a hidden talent . . . a gifting, if you will: the gift of interpreting dreams.

He'd actually started developing that skill when he lived at home with his siblings. In fact, sharing one of his own wild dreams had incited the jealousy of his brothers toward him. Turns out none of them wanted to hear about a time when they would bow down to Joseph like wheat.

Even after all the "wrong turns" Joseph had been on, God used him and his gift to help two fellow prisoners catch some z's. Only this was more than solving a mysterious dream; this was part of God's elaborate plan to eventually get Joseph in front of the right people at the right time.

Through another wild turn of events (I mean, it is Joseph, after all), one of those fellow prisoners, now newly free, called upon Joseph to help Pharaoh process some of his own bad dreams. Joseph gave insight and guidance to Pharaoh, breaking the news of an impending famine. He even advised Pharaoh on how to prepare to save the entire country from starving to death. Pharoah heeded the warning, and consequently, millions of lives were saved, all because Joseph had been in the right place (prison!) at the right time (after two years!) (Genesis 41:1).

Of course, it wasn't Joseph's warnings Pharaoh listened to—it was God's. God used Joseph's insightful gift of dream interpretation to save many lives. But Joseph had to be put in the perfect circumstances, which seemed completely imperfect at the time. A pit? A prison? Surely that's not the life God had planned for Joseph! Only it was. That was the set of circumstances God placed him in for his gift to be utilized and maximized to save the lives of innocent people from famine.

When all seemed lost, God was working for good what the Enemy had meant for evil (Genesis 50:20). We see Joseph stranded in a pit or tied up in a prison, and we want to swoop in and rescue him. We want to bust through the prison wall, find the key, and free him. But God placed him there in His sovereignty. He allowed Joseph to play a role in saving lives from famine, yes, but there is even more to his story.

Because of the famine, Joseph's brothers came to Egypt in dire need of food. They were shocked to discover that Joseph was in charge of Pharaoh's storehouses. In addition to getting the grain they needed to survive, Joseph and his brothers were given an opportunity to repair their broken relationship. The brothers repented, Joseph forgave them, and the family was reunited. That's the beauty of serving a sovereign God. We read Joseph's story and see a disaster, but God sees a way to put His glory on display and orchestrate something beautiful.

His Word tells us that His thoughts and ways are as far above ours as the heavens are higher than the earth (Isaiah 55:9). When life hands us circumstances that we can't make sense of, let's remember who God says He is: sovereign and good. This is when our faith and trust in Him must kick in—to catapult us into a place where, like Joseph, we continue to find favor in God's eyes because we believe God is who He says He is, even when it seems like the wheels may be falling off.

This may not make sense to us or to those around us, but welcome to the kingdom of God! It's like Opposite Day every day. Take everything you think and flip it upside down, and then you've nailed it. Want to lead? Be a servant. Want to be first? Make yourself last. Want to be free? Be willing to be chained.

What do you say we flip these earthly standards upside down and look through the lens of heaven? When we think we have every right to wallow and mourn, what if we choose to look to God and trust Him in the "prison" He's placed us in? May we use our circumstances to encourage others, continuing to utilize the gifts God has equipped us with . . . even when all appears lost and we feel forgotten by the world. May it be in those times that we remember even more fully that He is with us and He can be trusted to orchestrate all our circumstances for His glory and for our good.

CHAPTER FOUR

A Tale of Two Lifetimes

A person's a person, no matter how small.

DR. SEUSS[2]

When Jesus lived on the earth, He changed the way we keep track of time. He was *that* important. We mark all time by this one man. His existence was so monumental that the entire world decided that time *before* He arrived on the earth would be marked with one set of letters (BC), and time *after* His arrival would be marked with another set of letters (AD). The world follows these constraints of time even now, thousands of years after His appearance on earth.

Occasionally life affords us the opportunity to live two distinct lifetimes. That an event so remarkable, so earth-shattering, so life-changing would be enough to change the entire direction of our life's path is the reality some of us have found ourselves in—one lifetime marked by two distinct sets of letters.

I have lived two full lifetimes in the short span of my four decades on this planet. I mark time very clearly as *before diagnosis* and *after diagnosis*. One minute I was a young, naïve twenty-four-year-old girl, and the next I was picking up all the shattered, broken pieces of what felt like, at the time, a crushing blow.

I remember the day clearly. Two years into married life, Ryan and I felt the time was right to start a family. We wanted to be young, hip parents, so when we considered timelines for expanding our family, we figured the sooner the better. Pregnancy came easy for us, and before we knew it, we were eighteen weeks along with our first child and headed to our anatomy scan. If you're unfamiliar with the term, the anatomy scan is usually the most exciting pregnancy ultrasound. It's the one where gender is revealed (or concealed in an envelope for the now-popular gender reveal parties we see trending these days). We had intended to keep the gender of our baby a secret until the birth, so this appointment didn't hold as much anticipation as it would have if we'd planned to discover the gender. Though lacking anticipation, this scan certainly didn't lack excitement.

Lying there on the table while the technician scanned my ever-growing belly, I was thrilled to see our sweet little baby moving around on the screen. The technician took tons of measurements—to the point that it felt excessive. I was a first-time mom, but even I could tell this appointment was taking much longer than it should.

With curious eyes, the technician measured the baby's head, then abdomen, then head again, working diligently to collect data. Many long moments later, the measuring stopped, and she quietly stepped out to "go consult with the doctor."

In those moments of waiting, I reminded Ryan that I had felt something was off the entire day. Prior to our appointment, we had met at our townhome so we could carpool to the doctor's office. Standing in our kitchen, I voiced my fears. "What if something is wrong? What if the baby is missing an arm or something?" Ryan assured me I was being ridiculous and that everything would be fine. Yet here we were, sitting in awkward silence, wondering what the doctor would say. The tiny baby we had seen on the screen seemed beautiful, with a heart beating strongly. What more could there be to discuss?

My OB/GYN entered our room with a printout covered in numbers. Most were in black ink, but some were printed in red. We soon realized there was a reason red ink indicates errors not only on school papers but also on ultrasound printouts.

The doctor presented our "questionable results" from the day's scan. He explained that the abdominal measurements should match the head measurements, and both should represent the same number of weeks of gestation. However, the numbers printed in red revealed a head too small compared to the abdomen.

The doctor asked if there was a history of microcephaly in our families. Given that we had never heard that word before, we quickly answered with a firm no. Not being a specialist in the field of perinatology, our doctor referred us to a maternal fetal medicine specialist in Austin for further testing and interpretation of the results.

Our specialist appointment was set for the following Monday, the day after Easter. So I did what any sane, first-time mom would do: I spent the entire three-day weekend googling every single illness a baby in utero could have. After checking *microcephaly* first as my hottest lead, I threw in all combinations of verbiage that might help diagnose my baby. Zero stars. Do not recommend.

Ryan's parents were in town visiting us for the holiday weekend. We planned to have dinner Thursday night, spend time together on Good Friday, and attend church on Easter Sunday morning. On Thursday, I couldn't enjoy the chicken-fried steak I had ordered at our favorite hole-in-the-wall steak house. All I could think about was the internet research I had done and how much more I needed to do so I could be educated and equipped for what the specialist would reveal to us.

We finally confessed to Ryan's parents that our doctor's appointment had not been all we had hoped it would be. We shared the news of our uncertainty and reported that we would be going to Austin on Monday for additional scans and testing. Looking back now, I marvel at how their presence with us that weekend was God's provision. Having family to process with and be distracted by was a wonderful gift to one of the longest, most torturous weekends of our young married life.

My in-laws, never ones to shy away from a challenge, asked if they could accompany us to the appointment in Austin. We agreed that having them there for support would probably be wise. When receiving overwhelming news, it sometimes helps to have an extra pair of ears listening for key details that may be overlooked as we drown in stress and anxiety.

We arrived at our specialist appointment bright and early Monday morning, feeling nauseated and overwhelmed. Waiting in a room with other expectant moms, I couldn't help but scan the chairs and wonder if any of the women present felt as scared as I did. Or maybe they were further along on their journey than I was. They knew their diagnosis and plan, and I was the only one in the room who was lost and clueless. What brought them in today? How did they get to this place of sitting calmly in a perinatology waiting room?

Finally it was my turn to head back to a room and face whatever this was about to be. The doctor took another scan of my abdomen. This man, whom we had known for about two and a half minutes, held the ball in his court. Heck, he owned the court. We were seeking his expertise. We needed his knowledge and insight to help us understand what could be wrong with our baby.

The doctor led with a question. He asked if we had ever heard of spina bifida. I told him I was familiar with the term because I had interned for March of Dimes in college. Part of their mission is to educate women on the importance of folic acid while trying to conceive. According to the research at that time, folic acid supposedly helped prevent spina bifida and other neural tube defects—a fact I had learned and put into practice by taking the recommended dose of folic acid before conception. But a lot of good it was doing me now on this rainy day in Austin, learning that our baby had spina bifida despite my following all the rules and recommendations.

Spina bifida is a neural tube defect that occurs within the first twenty-eight days of gestation, and it happens in one of every 2,758 live births.[3] The term literally translates as "open spine." Essentially, when the baby's spinal cord is forming, it should close up nice and tight, like a zipper on a coat. But when a neural tube defect is present, the "zipper" doesn't close all the way. Just like what happens with a spinal cord injury, the higher up on the spinal cord the "open spine" happens, the more damage occurs to the systems in the body controlled by the nerves in that portion of the spinal cord. When the spinal cord touches the amniotic fluid, it irreversibly damages the spinal cord.[4]

The details of the in-utero diagnosis for our baby appeared to show a fairly positive scenario, all things considered. But that didn't make it easy. I was living *the* worst day of my young life, and I felt like a bystander watching it play out. It was surreal. I might as well have been having an out-of-body experience, hovering in the corner of the exam room, watching a young couple drown in overwhelming shock and grief.

The doctor explained what our next steps could be and outlined three options.

Option A: Do nothing, move forward with the pregnancy, educate ourselves on spina bifida, schedule a C-section (for the baby's safety), and deliver our child at a facility with a Level III NICU where the baby would go immediately after birth for treatment.

Option B: Option A plus perform an amniocentesis, an in-utero test that removes amniotic fluid from the womb and tests for further genetic anomalies that could be missed via ultrasound.

Option C: Terminate the pregnancy.

Three different choices, all of them difficult. If we chose to educate ourselves on this new diagnosis and raise a child with a severe disability, our lives would never be the same. If our baby died in-utero or at birth, I wasn't sure how I'd heal from that. If we chose to terminate our child's life, the pain of that tragedy would never go away. There is no handbook for how to walk through this uncharted territory.

After the doctor broke the news to the four of us, he and Ryan's parents stepped out of the room, and we were told to take all the time we needed. All the time we needed? I could've spent a lifetime in that tiny, dark room. Better yet, maybe there was a time machine hidden in a closet somewhere, and we could rewind time to back out of this whole thing.

None of this was what I had signed up for. It all sounded hard and messy, and it would be so much easier not to have to go through any of it. Running away, changing my identity, and escaping it all would have been easier than facing this challenge. But, as any woman who has been pregnant knows, it's a roller-coaster ride of its own, because one way or another, the child you carry in your body will eventually leave it.

Ryan and I stood in that exam room and sobbed. Two kids, twenty-four and twenty-five years old, holding on as tightly as we could to each other while the world around us went up in flames. I had never seen my young husband cry. There had been no reason for tears up until that day. Yet in the midst of our embrace was God and His Word and His steadfastness. In those solitary moments, after everyone stepped away, my marriage began the first of many morphing stages.

I remember playing bride as a little girl, wearing a pillowcase for a veil and daydreaming of what it would be like to be married. But you know what little girls don't dream of? Their new marriage suffering a devastating blow. Our new reality was that our firstborn child had a neural tube defect and would need immense care after birth and for a lifetime. This was the end of the marriage and life we had known. We were never going to be the couple we were ten minutes before meeting this doctor. No matter what the outcome was for our child or us, neither of us would ever be the same. Nor would our marriage.

I have to confess, when offered a variety of treatment options that afternoon, I spent a second too long considering the termination "treatment" option. (It's ludicrous that termination of pregnancy is called a treatment. And ridiculous for a doctor to recommended killing your child to "treat" him.) In the heat of the moment, when your entire world and all your lifelong hopes and dreams are burning to the ground, I think it's human nature to want the "easiest" solution, to make your problem disappear, even if for a split second.

In my opinion, part of that stems from First World problems. If you live in America, you have likely been exposed to the idea that your comfort and convenience come above all else. It's why we spend more money on cell phones than most people spent on their first cars a few decades ago. And why, if something is difficult or complicated, do we just "cancel" it, thinking our problems will vanish? Of course, they won't. They'll just present in other ways, sometimes as unaddressed trauma and even depression.

In that split-second instant where the rubber met the road, I almost forgot what it might cost me to live out my pro-life convictions. Oftentimes, an argument can be made for terminating a pregnancy if a child is diagnosed with a severe birth defect or an undesired diagnosis. Such a life-altering decision is not easy to make, certainly. I understand the gravity of holding the ability to choose when to end your child's life.

But each child conceived is a life God created in His infinite wisdom and goodness. And the truth is, we are all one diagnosis away from a life of inconvenience and immense suffering. If a spouse or child became an amputee, developed cancer, or became mentally handicapped following a motor vehicle accident, how do we respond? Do we look for ways to terminate their lives and limit our inconvenience? Or do we lean into God to glean all the wisdom we can from the scenario we're suddenly placed in? Where do we receive the strength to make these difficult decisions?

Putting pro-life into action that day, I looked at the ultrasound screen of the cutest little alien blob face and cried out to God in complete trust and surrender to Him and His plan. This was my time to decide if I truly believed it all. Did I believe the things I had learned about the Lord in twenty years of walking with Him? Did I believe that He was good no matter what? Did I trust His character? Did I believe that He would get me through whatever He called me to?

My husband and I fully knew that God could perform a miracle and that our baby could be born 100 percent fine. However, we also recognized that if God didn't do that, He had given us *this* baby, with *this* diagnosis, for a specific reason.

Life was affording me an opportunity to accept a challenge I never went looking for. I was given the chance to trust God and lay down my life for the sake of someone else. This was the scariest moment of my life, my biggest challenge to date. But for reasons I couldn't understand at that moment, this was the track God had set me on.

Our decision in that terrifying moment was to say yes. We would lean into our faith and trust Him to guide us down this new path, no matter how afraid we were. We knew our child with a diagnosis living inside my body would be no different from our child with a diagnosis living *outside* my body. We took Option C off the table.

Our next step was to move forward with Option B. We scheduled an amniocentesis for the following week, eager to learn all we could about our baby so we could develop the best plan of care for the birth and subsequent hospital stay. We also made the decision that since life had handed us enough surprises for one pregnancy, we would use the amniocentesis data to confirm the gender of the baby. To our delight, we learned we were having a little boy!

Have you had two lifetimes too? Was there a moment your life changed, ever after marked distinctly by that single event? Maybe it was a diagnosis, a death, or a decision. If you're a follower of Christ, perhaps your moment was when you were saved and sealed by the Holy Spirit. You can clearly see that the person you were before coming to Christ is distinctly different from the person you are now. Or could it be you are still searching for your lifetime moment—that up to now, you've lived as the same person, but you're ready to invite God to perform a transformation and change everything for you?

I can say now that receiving the news of our son's neural tube defect was extremely difficult for my husband and me, yet somehow also beautiful. Because at that minute, standing there in each other's arms and crying, no one else on this planet could explain what each of us felt. It's like being in a head-on collision in the same car with someone, and you both survive, and for the rest of your lives you tell everyone the miraculous story of how you walked away from the wreckage—not without bruises and cuts, but you walked away.

Hand in hand, Ryan and I walked out of that clinic united. Whatever happened with our son's life, we would handle it together, our arms wrapped around each other, with God in the center.

Johnna 37 weeks pregnant in Hayden's nursery in College Station, Texas, 2007

CHAPTER FIVE

Just Today

Suffering produces endurance.

ROMANS 5:3

When we find ourselves stuck living in a land of the impossible, where do we receive our strength? In the moments when every single part of our circumstance is difficult, how do we find the energy to do the next thing? There have been moments in my life when I have had to take one step at a time, in complete and pure exhaustion, willing my legs to place one foot in front of the other. Other times, all I could do was take a single breath and pray that God would grant me another breath to follow.

There's a popular Bible verse that says, "I can do all things through Christ who strengthens me" (Philippians 4:13 NKJV). I believe those words are true. But *how* is Christ strengthening us? Is it a one-and-done anointing, where once we come to know Jesus we are fully equipped to take on any struggle we encounter the rest of our days? Or is it a lifetime of being refined and learning to depend on His strength? The Word of God tells us that the dose of strength granted to us from Christ comes in daily doses.

You've probably had a prescription for an antibiotic filled at a pharmacy. When using any medication, we all know the importance of following the instructions on the label and taking the drug just as prescribed. The Bible also prescribes daily doses. Jesus Himself tells us in Matthew 6:34, "Sufficient for the day is its own trouble." The *day*. Not the week. Not the month. Not the toddler years. Not the course of chemo treatments. Not the stressful season you're in. The trouble is only for the *day*. We need not stress about the future but rather lean into God for the strength to survive today's burdens.

Jesus's disciples asked Him for advice on how to pray, and He taught them what we affectionately call the Lord's Prayer. In this prayer, Jesus asks the Father to "give us this day our daily bread" (Matthew 6:11). Even the Israelites, during their forty years in the desert, collected manna in jars and were told to gather it *daily* as a reminder that God's provisions are given to us each day. Lamentations 3:22–23 tells us, "His mercies . . . are new every morning"—not every quarter or on the first and fifteenth of every month, but each morning. God is so dependable and consistent that He will never miss a morning to hand out His mercies to His children.

Have you struggled with surrendering your day to God and asking Him to sustain you for the day? We are only called to live *today*. Tomorrow isn't even promised to us. So often we make the future an idol. We plan and dream and lose ourselves in a future we've designed, forgetting that God is already in tomorrow, working it for our good and for His glory. Can we trust Him in that? Can we believe that He is good and that He can sustain us for the day He has created? Can we utilize the breath He placed in our lungs to glorify Him and bring Him honor?

$$\infty$$

In the Old Testament, an Israelite named Daniel was a follower of Yahweh. In his teenage years (most likely), he was dragged out of his tribe of Judah in Jerusalem and taken, against his will, to Babylon. Years before, God had used a prophet, Jeremiah, to warn His people that they would be taken into captivity for seventy years because of their rebellion, and when we meet Daniel on the pages of Scripture, we see God fulfilling that prophecy.

Daniel was from the royal family, and because of that, he piqued the interest of the Babylonian king, Nebuchadnezzar. Ol' King Neb was searching out people with potential, specifically "youths without blemish, of good appearance and skillful in all wisdom, endowed with knowledge, understanding learning, and competent to stand in the king's palace" (Daniel 1:4). Talk about having the full package! Daniel and his closest friends met all of these standards, and so they were taken to Babylon, where King Nebuchadnezzar intended to train the captives to become court advisers.

Given a new Babylonian name, Belteshazzar, Daniel was taught a new language and literature. These changes were an attempt to alter Daniel's biblical worldview into a Babylonian one. However, though his surroundings had changed, Daniel's relationship and commitment to God did not. Daniel made certain, no matter the location or culture, that he kept to his daily prayer vigil, followed his convictions regarding food and drink, and never lost faith in his God.

One of those first life-changing moments in his new surroundings was during a dinner in Babylon. The Israelite captives were allowed to eat and drink like kings (score!) and be educated in Babylonian ways for three years, and then they would stand before the king. There was one problem, though, and it was a biggie. The menu made for kings didn't line up with God's menu for His people, according to the laws given to them by Moses (e.g., don't eat food offered to idols).

To honor God and avoid defiling himself, Daniel approached the staff member in charge of the captives' indoctrination and asked if he and his Hebrew buddies could have a reprieve from the king's table. Instead, they would drink only water and eat only vegetables as a ten-day test, after which Daniel and his friends' health would be assessed. God was with Daniel, just like He had been with Joseph. The Bible says, "God gave Daniel favor and compassion," and his request was granted (Daniel 1:9).

When the time came for the ten-day "Daniel Fast" to begin (What a trendsetter Daniel was!), I believe that Daniel took it one day at a time. When the salad bar opened up right beside the meat buffet, he had a choice to make. Daniel was committed to following God's commands, even in what seemed like the small things, such as meal times, but his commitment to food laws went deeper. He was dedicated to honoring God's laws, no matter what the local law said.

Isn't that how those of us committed to following Jesus are called to live? We have to be faithful in our walk and trust that God will make provisions for us daily. That when everyone around us in our Babylon is sacrificing to the pagan gods of work, status, body image, and raising well-behaved Olympic-athlete children, we stand up and declare that, at least for today, we will not let this world defile us.

Not only do we need to choose to obey, we also have to rely on God's favor and compassion in equipping us to follow His commands.

We cannot do any of this on our own. It's in our weakness that His power is made strong in us.

~~~

Daniel spent the better part of forty years in Babylon. He served the Babylonian government faithfully with a spotless record. But that was just his day job. Daniel continued to follow God and His laws with unwavering faith. Imagine the faith it would take to spend four decades of your life exiled from your church family, your hometown, and your local Costco, but never giving up on God . . . no matter how much indoctrination was thrown at you. In all the distractions and difficulties on his journey, Daniel never veered from the path God had laid out for him.

Leaders came and went during Daniel's time in Babylon. After King Nebuchadnezzar, his relative Belshazzar took over. And still, Daniel remained committed to serving Babylon with integrity. Belshazzar's rule ended with an invisible hand and a wild graffiti night (Daniel 5:5), and shortly thereafter, his death, making way for the next king in line to show up, King Darius (Daniel 5:31). Still, Daniel's reputation remained spotless. He even got a promotion, which caused his fellow politicians to become quite jealous.

Because Daniel's reputation was one of noble character, he had become a nuisance to the Babylonian leaders serving alongside him. In an effort to put an end to Daniel and all his favor with King Darius, a group of men came up with a plan to back Daniel into a catch-22 situation. Once they had Daniel trapped, they would have him exterminated, removing this thorn from their side. Daniel's reputation preceded him, and these guys felt confident this plan would certainly put an end to Daniel.

After a bit of lip service, the high officials, prefects, satraps, counselors, and governors of Babylon asked King Darius to sign an ordinance and injunction that "whoever petitions any god or man for thirty days, except you, O king, shall be cast into the den of lions" (Daniel 6:7 NKJV). For a pagan king who trusted the staff around him, this sounded like a fine idea. So King Darius, trusting a little too much that his staff members were making wise decisions, gave his signature and put the decree into action—a decision that could not be revoked. And thus the sinister plan was set into motion.

When word of this new edict got around, Daniel didn't pay it any mind. Daniel 6:10 says the first thing he did when he heard the news about this law and its consequences was to go home, and with the windows wide open, he "got down on his knees three times a day and prayed and gave thanks before his God, as he had done previously." Knowing full well he could be lion's food at any moment, Daniel chose faith over fear. He continued in his routine of praying daily to God and giving thanks.

Daniel was receiving his daily bread. He was thanking his Father and asking for his manna. The amount of courage and faith in God's goodness that Daniel had to be able to fight the culture and break an edict is remarkable. We don't know for certain how many days this went on before Daniel was caught praying, but once the men observed him and reported him to the king, Daniel's fate was sealed. Off to the den of lions he went. Though King Darius was distressed over this news and had "set his mind to deliver Daniel" (Daniel 6:14), there was nothing to be done to stop it—at least nothing an earthly king could do.

Daniel's heavenly King, however, did not abandon Daniel. God sent His angel to shut the lions' mouths, leaving Daniel unharmed. "No kind of harm was found on him, because he had trusted in his

God" (Daniel 6:23). Not a scratch, not a hairball, not a tear of his cloak.

After a night of having their mouths shut by angels, the lions were starving. The men who had set up Daniel, along with their children and wives, were cast to the lions and were gone before they even reached the bottom of the den.

When we're dragged off to our own Babylon and cast into a den of hungry lions, God won't abandon us. He puts the breath into our lungs. Take a big breath right now. Feel that? That's a gift directly to you from the Creator of the universe, who holds all things together in His hands. "As long as I have life within me, the *breath of God* [is] *in my nostrils*" (Job 27:3 NIV, emphasis mine). We can trust the Author of Life to be present with us daily, sustaining us.

This life will try to overtake you. This world and the prince of it, Satan, don't want you to succeed in the plans God has for you. If you're following Jesus, the Prince of Darkness wants you defeated and fed to the lions. In love, God warns us in His Word to "be sober-minded; be watchful. Your adversary the devil prowls around like a roaring lion, seeking someone to devour" (1 Peter 5:8). Let me remind you that you have a real enemy. But he loses! Jesus overcame death and defeated Satan once and for all. And if you know Jesus, you share in that same victory because Jesus made a way for you to be redeemed—to be free. "It is for freedom that Christ has set us free" (Galatians 5:1 NIV).

The remaining six chapters of Daniel, following the attempt on his life, shift into prophecy about end-times events. (Did you know there's more about the end times and the apocalypse than just what we find in the book of Revelation? I told you the Bible is a must-read!) Could it be that the Enemy tried to shut down Daniel, using the mouths of lions and a deceitful decree created out of jealousy, in hopes of stopping the end-times prophecy from being told? Especially prophecies that show Satan's ultimate demise.

What has the Enemy tried to ruin or shut down in your life? Has he dominated your marriage with unrealistic fears that your spouse will find someone better and abandon you? Has he tricked you into believing that it's impossible for you to attend college and break generational strongholds? Or maybe he's convinced you that you don't deserve a healthy child, and that's why your son has been given a challenging diagnosis. Isn't it time we remind the Enemy that with our daily dose of manna, we will walk into victory, no matter how many odds are stacked against us, knowing full well that Jesus will sustain us?

I was learning my own lesson of not growing weary. I didn't know it yet, but seeking God's daily manna and provision was about to be the only thing that would sustain me for the day, and oftentimes, the minute.

CHAPTER SIX

210 Days

Never be afraid to trust an unknown future to a known God.

—CORRIE TEN BOOM

On August 3, 2007, all the fetal MRIs, ultrasounds, amniocentesis, and tears were a distant memory as my husband and I laid our eyes on our beautiful, six-pound, two-ounce little boy. Hayden came into the world quietly, without a cry or sound, but he was breathing and present with us. He and I both had surgery on the same day—mine left me with a C-section scar marking his safe arrival; his, a scar on his back to close the gaping hole he arrived with.

At each prenatal appointment with our specialized team in Houston, my OB/GYN always reminded me that no matter what happened after giving birth, this was still *my* baby. I thought it was a silly reminder. Obviously I knew this was my baby. I made him. He would literally be coming out of my body. But when my son was taken away from me moments after delivery and sent to the children's hospital next door for treatment while I was half-conscious in recovery, I remembered those words from the doctor. This was *my* baby. It was now my job to advocate for him, to speak up and ask questions, and to ensure he was being taken care of in the best way possible.

Lying in my postpartum hospital bed alone with only the hum of a breast pump keeping me company, while my baby and husband were at another hospital, I felt like Daniel. This was my exile. But instead of being dragged off to Babylon against my will, I had been sent to a lonely, quiet postpartum room with no baby in sight.

You've seen the "All Sales Final" sign posted in stores, right? It means if you buy something, you'd better be prepared to stick with it because there are no takebacks. That's parenthood, isn't it? When you have a child, you're in a no-returns situation. "You get what you get, and you don't throw a fit." Becoming first-time NICU parents didn't just feel like we'd been thrown into the deep end of the parenting pool. We found ourselves in the middle of the ocean during a hurricane . . . with no life vests and sharks circling.

∽

Following surgery, patients are encouraged to get out of bed and walk to build strength and to prevent blood clots from forming. My mother-in-law accompanied me on a lap around the postpartum unit the morning after Hayden's delivery. We took a break near the nursery window full of "healthy babies" on display and bawled our eyes out right along with the babies, thinking of how much we wished Hayden was with us instead of in a NICU. While most babies enjoy skin-to-skin bonding with their mothers minutes after birth, Hayden spent his first moments in the world lying alone on a sterile operating room table, having his back sewn shut to stop the leaking of cerebrospinal fluid from the defect in his spine.

Falling to sleep each night during my hospital stay to the sounds of my neighbor's baby crying at her breast was not the way I wanted to be welcomed into motherhood. Yet here I was, twenty-four years old, in the midst of fighting a battle I never signed up for but was drafted into. And I wasn't the only one—Hayden had been chosen to fight in this battle as well. And fight he did, quite well, I might add.

Four days after giving birth, it was time for my discharge from the hospital. Since we had chosen to deliver in Houston, we were displaced from our home in College Station, ninety-five miles away. We utilized a nearby nonprofit facility called Ronald McDonald House for room and board during Hayden's hospitalization.

Leaving the hospital days after major surgery without my baby was terrible. I slowly and gently crawled into the car, trying not to disturb the staples in my abdomen, while through tears I peeked at the empty car seat where my child should be, and as my husband drove off, I left half of my heart behind. We weren't driving home to climb into our own beds where I could handle postpartum bleeding, healing, and crying, though. We drove to a strange place with an unfamiliar bed, a community kitchen, and a laundromat.

The night we checked into RMH, a volunteer group served families a lovely meal they'd brought. In physical and emotional pain, as I stood in line to receive a plate, I was surrounded by children who were bald from fighting ferociously against cancer and other strangers living out battles just like we were. I wasn't sure I would survive any of it—the meal, the healing of my body, the hospitalization journey we were embarking on. How does a person find the strength to wake up each day and fight? I was homeless, recovering from surgery and childbirth, and baby-less.

Each day in a neonatal ICU is an exhausting, emotional roller coaster ride. You learn to take each hour as it comes. A lot of babies go to the NICU because they're premature and need time to grow. Hayden was born full term, so he wasn't there to grow—he was there to heal. His first day of life brought his first surgery, and he had ten more surgeries before his eventual discharge.

My husband and I gradually settled into our daily hospital routine. Each morning we sat in on rounds with the team of neonatologists and a resident who kicked off each morning meeting with "This is Baby Boy Hensley. Day of life number ___." I had no idea on "Day of life number 1" that we would eventually count all the way up to 210.

Seven full months we lived life day by day, hour by hour. We spent my twenty-fifth and Ryan's twenty-sixth birthdays, Thanksgiving, Christmas, New Year's Eve, our third wedding anniversary, Valentine's Day, and an entire Texas Aggie football season in NICU space A17. Each morning, I packed a lunch from the Ronald McDonald House community kitchen and gathered my things to stay at Hayden's bedside from 7:00 a.m. until 10:30 p.m., taking breaks only to pump breast milk, which he received through a feeding pump that slowly dripped tiny quantities through his gastrostomy tube into his fragile stomach.

Eventually, Ryan had to go back to work, of course. He left each weekday morning for his ninety-minute commute to College Station. He returned each night to help with Hayden's bath-time routine and to spend time together as a family. Tirelessly providing for his family,

Ryan never complained once over the dozen weeks of juggling work and having a hospitalized child.

Two months into Hayden's hospitalization, we were informed of the medical necessity for a tracheostomy—an airway created surgically with a hole in his neck and into his trachea. Since his brain struggled to tell his lungs when to breathe, a machine would be hooked up to his body to help him breathe. Up to this point, we had tried every intervention, including surgeries, to prevent the need for a tracheostomy. Alas, the only way we were going to be able to take our child home was with this surgically created stable airway in place.

I sat in the hallway with the neonatologist on rotation for the month, Dr. Fernandes. I confessed through tears, "I don't want my baby to have a trach—but I want to go home." He comforted me and calmed my fears, reminding me that the trach may not be forever and that lots of patients have them removed as they grow and develop over time.

The pressure to make wise medical decisions for our child was heavy. With a shaky hand and tears in my eyes, I signed consent for the procedure, which would be performed a few days after Hayden turned two months old.

The tracheostomy surgery was a success, and we thought Hayden was healing well. But the following week things took a turn for the worse. Hayden became severely ill and septic, with an unknown infection ravaging his body.

I described what was happening in a blog post I wrote to our family and friends on October 18, 2007:

His kidneys still aren't working properly because he's not getting enough blood to them, so they're not making much urine. He's not draining off any of the fluids he's getting through his central line and his new IV they placed last night. Today's goal is to get the kidneys working better. . . .

They gave him blood and other blood-clotting products. They also placed another arterial line so they could get an accurate blood pressure on him. He's now getting fentanyl on a drip to keep him knocked out and help with pain. He's also on dopamine to regulate his blood pressure and concentrate the blood in his veins better. The dopamine should help bring his heart rate down, which had been at 220 most of the night last night. He's normally at 144–160s. . . .

Sorry to report such bad news. . . . Please pray for Hayden. He does not look well, and I know he doesn't feel good at all. Please lift us all up. I apologize if this is a bit choppy. . . . So much is happening right now.

The hospital shut down the NICU from outside visitors so the pediatric surgeon could operate on Hayden at his bedside, since transporting him to the operating room was too risky. I remember each detail from that day: where I stood in the hallway as I called Ryan while he was at work and each set of grandparents, saying, "Get to Houston—*now!*" I remember the intense fear of thinking I was about to lose my baby. Above all, I remember being on my knees, pleading with God not to take Hayden.

Until this point in our NICU journey, I'd prayed lukewarm prayers. I told our prayer warriors what to pray for, but it felt like none of those requests would be answered in the way we hoped. It seemed as if God was doing the opposite of what I asked. I felt frustrated and tired, and my hope was fading—until that night.

Ryan arrived from College Station, and we met together in one of the hard-to-come-by private pumping rooms in the milk bank. We were processing the nightmare we were in the middle of and praying. I got down on my knees and pleaded for God not to take my baby. The exact words of my prayer were, "I don't care *how* hard it will be in this life, *please* don't take my baby from me."

While we signed yet another surgical consent form, the pediatric surgeon told us Hayden had a fifty-fifty chance of surviving the exploratory surgery she was about to perform. She had no idea what she would find when she opened his distended abdomen. What other choice did we have but to proceed with the surgery and discover if there was anything to be done to help him?

She discovered that Hayden had a mesenteric venous thrombosis—a blood clot in his intestines—and because of that, his small intestines had not received any blood flow and had died, leaving a septic, infected baby boy. That night, Hayden lost forty-three centimeters of his small intestines to the blood clot, but he was expected to survive. We had a lifetime of gastroenterology appointments, specialty formulas, constant monitoring, and lab draws ahead of us, but our child would live. God had heard my cry and answered my prayer.

∽∾

As the weeks progressed, we came to understand more fully what it would be like to live outside the hospital and to raise a child with a tracheostomy, a ventilator, and short bowel syndrome. Hayden would need a plethora of doctors and nurses to help him thrive. Children like Hayden require constant monitoring and intervention by nursing staff in the home health setting.

Accepting this new reality, we decided it would be best to put our College Station home on the market, with its beautiful and perfectly prepared nursery that our son would never see, and begin our new life in Houston, near Texas Children's Hospital.

Hayden had been in the NICU for around four months, with no discharge date in sight, when we rented a one-bedroom apartment in the Texas Medical Center. Since our house was staged for sale, the only belongings we took with us to our apartment were an ice chest for a table, lawn chairs for seating, and an air mattress to complete our main bedroom suite. At night we fell asleep to the hum of a deep freezer in our bedroom filled to the brim with pumped breast milk (which Hayden couldn't even use now due to his new GI condition—oh, the irony).

I used to believe that because I was not able to choose my life circumstances, the ones I ended up with were second rate. But now I realize that I do have a choice. I get to decide how to respond to the life I have. I am allowed to choose whether to embrace a chaotic life I hadn't planned on or stall out and wallow in the life I ended up with. In the difficult moments, I think of Daniel, who, being exiled from all that he knew, chose to respond in faith and embrace the situation God had placed him in.

I've come to learn that when you're broken, God has more pieces to work with. Becoming the parent of a chronically ill and disabled child broke me into a million tiny pieces. But as with Kintsugi art, we can see the value of broken pieces during reconstruction. In this Japanese art tradition, broken pottery is pieced and glued back together using gold, enhancing the beauty of what was once considered broken and valueless. When put back together using gold as the adhesive, these broken, chipped bits and pieces create a beautiful artwork that could not have been created if not for the broken parts. I was broken and shattered, but God was building me back with gold.

I now treasure life in a way I never would have before experiencing these trials. I have a fresh perspective. And I have a daily opportunity to live out sacrificial love and to die to self. I will never again look at situations, circumstances, or "stuff" the same way.

As Christ followers, our identity is in Jesus—not in the things we own, the clothes we wear, the jobs we have, or the vacations we take. None of this defines us. Christ does. If all the things in your life disappear, will you allow Him to be your unchanging rock and steady fortress?

The NICU roller coaster taught us that when life throws curveballs, it's an opportunity to reevaluate priorities. Although we were incredibly grateful to have had the gift of affordable housing with close proximity to the hospital, we welcomed a change from the community living setup we used for four months at the Ronald McDonald House. We appreciated all the more our own space, our own kitchen, and the freedom to come and go without checking in with a front desk.

Within the bare-bones walls of our eight-hundred-square-foot apartment, I began to see the specks of gold shining through my broken heart. I understood that the size of your home, the make and model of your car, or the number of zeros on your paycheck mean nothing when stacked against the sanctity of life. Fighting a life-or-death battle shifts your perspective in ways nothing else can.

Hayden's birth and NICU journey was just the beginning of our refinement as a couple, as a family, and, most importantly, as followers of Jesus. We were placed in a position that truly enabled our hearts to be molded to God's calling . . . to leave everything behind and seek after Him. And that part of our adventure was just beginning.

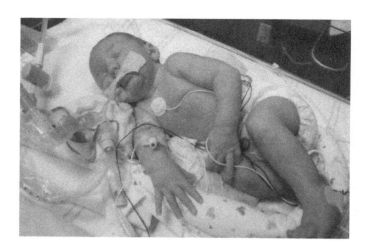

*Hayden, Day of Life 5, NICU at Texas Children's Hospital
in Houston, Texas, August 2007*

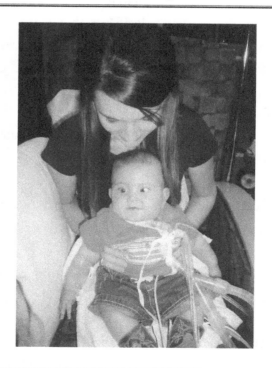

*Hayden, Day of Life 209, NICU at Texas Children's Hospital
in Houston, Texas, February 2008*

CHAPTER SEVEN

In Light of Eternity

Endurance produces character.

ROMANS 5:4

For many Christians, there comes a moment in our walk with the Lord when we are tested and we have to decide what we truly believe about God and our faith. I've had quite a few of those moments, and I'll bet you have too. When the rug is pulled out from under us, and we're left in a twisted-up pile of confusion and frustration, we wonder why God would let tragedies and disappointments happen to us if He loves us as much as He alleges.

Processing those moments looks different for each of us. I confess that in the early years of my relationship with God, I couldn't understand why He wasn't granting my requests as I thought He should, especially when I had followed the "Christian formula" to the letter. I prayed for the right things, I treated people fairly, I attended Bible studies, and I served at my church . . . but I gave birth to a child who would need major medical interventions for his entire life. My spiritual calculator kept giving me an error message. Surely something was wrong with this formula!

And then I realized I was after God's stuff, not God. I wanted ease in the temporal instead of living for eternity.

Sitting too long in the disappointments of my earthly losses left me fixated on earthly things—not the desire for trinkets and toys but for all my struggles, pain, and difficulties to be removed. I had made an "easier life" my idol. All the while I was missing the beautiful, eternal value in my challenging, earthly circumstances.

Part of this realization comes when we begin to live our lives with the right perspective. Having an eternal perspective instead of a carnal, worldly perspective is crucial to understanding God's plan for His people. The world would have you believe living for eternity is foreign and backward.

We live in a time when everything around us makes keeping an eternal perspective nearly impossible. We are a microwave generation. We wait for nothing. If our home internet is running slowly, we drive to our local coffee shop to use their Wi-Fi. If we don't get immediate "likes" and positive feedback on our social media posts, we are crushed. Our text messages and emails hunt us down on our "smart" devices, and there's no longer a need to eagerly anticipate receiving written correspondence from a friend. "Me, me, me" and "now, now, now" are the lyrics to our theme song these days.

The prince of this fallen world, our Enemy, will shine flashy things in our faces: status, wealth, pleasure, and ease. But it is actually possible to set our minds "on things that are above" (Colossians 3:2) when we seek the Word of God, learn His ways, and draw close to Him.

And sometimes our eternal perspective is gifted to us through the difficult circumstances of our earthly lives.

∞

A Bible character named Job comes onto the scene a few hundred years after the flood in Genesis. The book of Job opens with a scene in the heavenlies where God and His angels are having a conference, and Satan is permitted to attend. When asked what he's been up to, Satan reports that he's been "going to and fro on the earth, and from walking up and down on it" (Job 1:7). Let this serve as a friendly reminder that our enemy is out on the prowl, looking for "someone to devour" (1 Peter 5:8).

God submits to Satan to consider Job, His humble servant, who fears God and is committed to Him. Satan casts doubt on Job's integrity by suggesting the only reason he is living his life to honor God is that God gives him blessings. This is the Name-It-and-Claim-It, Blab-It-and-Grab-It concept that is very much alive today, often called the prosperity gospel. We could think of this practice as a math problem: if A, then B. *If I go to church every Sunday and tithe at least 10 percent of my income, then God will protect my children and myself from injury or harm, and we will be blessed.* Job has three friends who ascribe to this type of thinking, and they use this theory when they attempt to counsel Job.

Lest we forget, God's ways are not our ways, and we can't just plug in some holy formula and expect a particular outcome. What type of faith would that be? I would submit to you an even heavier question to consider: Are you after God or just His stuff?

In the heavenly meeting, God granted Satan permission to intervene in Job's circumstances—to a degree. He was not allowed to take Job's life, but everything else was fair game. God warns Satan that Job will remain faithful to Him. Even so, Satan brings calamity down upon him. Job loses nearly everything—his children, his livestock, and his health. But he never loses the correct perspective of God and eternity.

Job says, "Naked I came from my mother's womb, and naked shall I return. The LORD gave, and the LORD has taken away; blessed be the name of the LORD" (Job 1:21). When his life was in shambles, Job's wife suggested he "curse God and die" (Job 2:9). Instead, Job doubled down on who he understood God to be. He recognized that all he had to begin with came from God, so it was His to take away. And through it all, he praised the name of the Lord.

Job's response of integrity is not the norm these days. The minute something inconvenient unfolds, we tend to panic, scream that we're "triggered," and jump ship on our day, our walk, our purpose.

Have you had one of those moments? I can admit I have been there been plenty of times. In the small inconveniences and in the large, life-shattering moments, I have wanted to throw my hands up and call it quits on trusting God's plan. This is a normal human reaction and part of the process and cycle of grief.

Grief is not a virus that merely lasts seven to ten days before your body becomes immune to it. It is with you constantly, though it may lie dormant for windows of time as you begin to process and heal. But you're never fully cured.

Merriam-Webster's definition of grief is "deep and poignant distress caused by or as if by bereavement."[5] I used to think you could only grieve a dead person. I now know you can grieve a living person. I grieved the loss of the marriage and life I thought I would have, the loss of a healthy, able-bodied child, the loss of ease and freedom, and the loss of carefree parenting.

But in my grief, I was struck with my own depravity. I realized it was by God's grace that I had been given anything at all. After Hayden's birth and seven-month hospitalization, I entered into a cycle of sin, so much so that I didn't even recognize myself in the mirror anymore. The Enemy tried hard to use the diagnosis and hospital stay to destroy me, my marriage, and my calling. When that tactic didn't work, he went for the jugular: an attack on me from the inside out. And I fell for it.

I would like to blame it on all the trauma I had endured or the exhaustion I was under or the hunger for an escape from the difficult reality of life with a disabled child. But the truth is that I fell into sin because I didn't have God on the throne of my life. I let circumstances and survival become an idol and placed them above my love for God and His sovereignty over my life. Unlike Job, I was not a person of complete integrity who feared God and turned away from evil (Job 1:1 NLT). Yet I wanted to be. So badly.

Surely I'm not the only one. Have you woken up one day faced with the realization that you have no idea how you got to where you are, but all you know is you need a way out? Then you look up with clarity and see Jesus standing right there with His arms outstretched, waiting for you to reunite with Him. He never left. His arms were never closed to you. He welcomes you back into His embrace, even after sin and rebellion and idolatry.

I ran into His arms, held on tightly, and have never let go since. It took my moment of awakening and complete depravity to realize I had let this world, and the prince of it, distract me from my purpose here on earth. The Enemy worked in overdrive to stop me from something great, even though I couldn't envision it at the time. But all that running Satan did was done with God's permission. And as his running came to an end, God drew me back to Him. I stepped down from the throne of my own life, realizing that all I had was His. I came into this world naked, and I'll leave it the same way.

I still mourn not getting to know Ryan as a dad to only typically developing children—a life where he's the Little League coach and has free time and hobbies and a life outside of just keeping our son alive. I am often curious about how different our marriage would be if our life wasn't built around discussing medical supply orders, nursing staff changes, and scheduling doctor appointments.

Each August, I'm filled with mounds of grief when I see Hayden's classmates moving on with their age-appropriate lives during back-to-school season—when they're on the football field running and joking around with one another after practice and when best friendships are formed. It saddens me that my son doesn't have a best friend. I grieve the fun we could've had as a family not held down by catheterization schedules and breathing treatments. There's no room for impromptu loosey-goosey fun when health takes precedence and a stringent hourly calendar must be kept.

There are plenty of things in this life I will grieve until the end of my days. But there's beauty as well. There's been tremendous healing and incredible amounts of love shared. Through this set of less-than-ideal (from an earthly perspective) circumstances, God brought about true, deep healing in myself. And through our family and my son, there has been healing for many others around us.

I know I would have dearly loved my "husband of only healthy children." Because in this hard and difficult journey we walk together, he is a fabulous dad. He supports our family with grace and endurance. I thank God I get to run this race with him by my side.

∞

For nearly the rest of the book of Job, we read a back-and-forth conversation between him and his friends. Initially these friends have appropriate responses to Job's loss and pain. For seven days, they sit in silence with Job (Job 2:13). Oftentimes, when we find ourselves in trials, that's all we really need . . . a friend to sit in the sadness with us, being present but quiet. The Bible instructs us to "weep with those who weep" (Romans 12:15 NKJV).

After the seven days, the friends take turns speaking with Job using their human ideas to brainstorm reasons for Job's suffering. They assume that surely it's because of his sin that he finds himself in such a predicament.

Their conversations with one another go on for twenty-eight chapters until, finally, God speaks to Job directly through a whirlwind. During their talk, God asks Job a variety of questions, and Job is humbled. Up to this point, Job had been pondering why God had afflicted him. God's response reminded him of God's sovereignty and power in all things. God asked Job, "Where were you when I laid the foundation of the earth?" (Job 38:4). Job was reminded that it's God who had made the world. It's God who brings the sunrise each morning, stirs the wind, and makes the stars shine and lightning bolts strike.

Job recognized his error in questioning God's motives for allowing his trials. And in true humility, he repented for questioning what God was allowing in his life. Job had been interested in *why* things were happening to him, but God was more interested in showing *who* was in control in the midst of the chaos.

During our own times of tribulation, of which there are sure to be plenty, may we pray that God would use our trials to help us see Him better, understand Him more, and grow deeper in our relationship with Him.

The idea of worshiping God through a disaster seems foreign to some. Why bother to praise a God who allows suffering and pain and death to rain down on your family? That seems like a tall order to ask of someone in great pain. If you're full of faith and committed to trusting God's goodness and sovereignty in all circumstances, that's wonderful! Or perhaps you used to have the same kind of commitment Job had, but then your circumstances became so unbearable that they broke you, and you've walked away from God and the close relationship you used to treasure. Maybe you're somewhere in between. I've found myself in all of those places at different points in my life.

Trusting God in every circumstance was a lesson I had been continuously learning the hard way. Until now, the circumstances had been less than ideal. But all that was about to change . . . for the better.

CHAPTER EIGHT

First-Time Mom. Again.

*Sometimes ... fear does not subside and ...
one must choose to do it afraid.*

ELISABETH ELLIOT

When Hayden left the hospital for the first time after seven long months, the taste of freedom was incredibly sweet. It didn't take long to settle into a daily routine on our own of completing all of his medical treatments, feedings, catheterizations, and therapies. It felt like a treat to be outside the hospital walls, enjoying our child and watching him be a baby! We transitioned from our tiny apartment, where Hayden's bedroom had been the breakfast nook, and settled into a house in the Houston suburbs, with enough space for all our medical supplies and baggage.

Hayden qualified for home health nursing care with constant coverage due to his intense medical diagnosis and ventilator dependence. However, he was my only child, and I decided to play the role of "Stay-at-Home Mom 2.0" by being with him as his mom and also as his nurse during the day. (We did accept nursing help during overnight hours so we could sleep, trusting he was being closely monitored for any emergencies.) Though he was sick often and inpatient occasionally, for the most part Hayden did well outside of the hospital.

I was working a full-time gig with Hayden as his mom, nurse, and physical, occupational, and speech therapist, and the joy of my life was watching him learn and grow. I made it my mission to show the world how smart my son was. Due to his vocal cord paralysis and tracheostomy, Hayden was nonverbal, but he learned American Sign Language like a champ. We began teaching it to him while he was in the NICU. The day he turned six months old, I had stepped away from Hayden's bedspace for a quick moment but then received a text from Ryan saying Hayden was asking for me. He had made the sign for "Mommy" while I was gone to make his requests known!

I spent most of my waking moments trying to further develop that intelligence in him and display it to the world. I made videos of him using our Picture Exchange Communication System (PECS)[6] to teach functional communication so he could let us know his needs. I recorded in a journal all of his physical therapy milestones, his progress with touching different textures to overcome sensory processing issues, and his ability to identify shapes and sort them. His thriving was my entire focus and consumed each minute of my day. And I loved it. I treasured our time together, and no one else on this planet could understand him more than I could. The two of us had a beautiful, unique, deep bond.

When Hayden was eighteen months old, Ryan and I began discussing when and if we would make the leap from one child to two. That's when "normal" families had more kids. You know, the perfect two years apart and stair stepped set of well-behaved children in monogrammed smocks? Of course, we knew that would never be us. Which is fine, because I look terrible in smocked rompers.

Ryan was convinced we should have more children. His mind was decided, and all he needed was for both of us to be on the same page. Except we weren't on the same page. Not even the same bookshelf. After thirty weeks in the NICU, I had seen much more than my eyes had ever bargained for, and I couldn't erase those images from my mind. I knew too much and had learned about conditions I never knew existed; ignorance was no longer bliss. I could never forget the many babies and families we saw daily in the NICU, only to never see them again when the unthinkable happened. Too many families left the NICU empty-handed.

I couldn't erase the pain and fear and hurt and anguish that we'd experienced in our NICU time. This journey had affected me deeply and probably left me with significant PTSD. I can still smell the soap from the sinks and hear the sounds of the hospital ventilator alarm— memories that are rooted deep in my subconscious.

When Ryan asked if I was ready to expand our family, I said I didn't want any more children. I couldn't risk it. He seemed to have forgotten all we had witnessed in the NICU. Good for him. But I was not open to the idea in the slightest. Even after all we had been through, I had not learned to fully let go of control and trust God. I still wanted to captain my own ship. You'd think I would have figured out this wasn't the best option! But nope—I wanted to avoid risk and take the safest route possible, even if it meant skipping out on giving Hayden siblings. Besides, Hayden and I had a good thing going, and adding more children could interrupt our vibe. It was a gamble I didn't want to take.

One day, as I stood in our bathroom getting ready for the day, I heard the Lord speak to me—not audibly, but as clear as any thought I've ever had. He told me, "Whatever child you get is for *My* glory, not yours." In that moment, everything changed. I understood I was selfishly holding out on bringing God glory through whatever children and circumstances He gave us. I was not trusting Him fully in all things. I was trying to avoid the roller-coaster ride instead of trusting the Operator.

In that moment I surrendered to God's direction. I chose to believe Him and trust Him. He had told me that whatever child He gave to us was for His glory. Who was I to stand in His way?

∽

Not long after that life-altering interaction with the Spirit, I got pregnant with our second child. Because of our past medical history with Hayden, I was fast-tracked to be followed by a maternal fetal medicine doctor and grouped into a high-risk category. Although the doctor who would deliver this second baby was the same, I hoped and prayed that the experience wouldn't be. Hayden's birth experience was chaotic, painful, and sad. I looked forward to redeeming all of that this second go-around.

My husband and I took Bradley Method[7] natural childbirth classes with a small group of expectant parents. We chose that method because it supports delivering a baby with the least amount of medical interventions possible—my number-one wish given all we had gone through during Hayden's birth. During pregnancy, mothers follow intentional breathing and relaxation strategies to prepare their bodies for birth with minimal intervention and no pain medication at delivery. We hired a doula, a labor and birth support specialist, who was a phenomenal aid to us.

On Halloween night 2010, I was out trick-or-treating with Hayden, who was wearing a Wheel of Fortune costume, an ode to his favorite TV game show. I had painted wedges from the famous wheel to cover his wheelchair tires, along with a glittery $5,000 wedge for him to wear around his neck.

My costume, you ask? Oh, I was "Woman in Labor." Literally. Every five to seven minutes I stopped on the sidewalk to process through a contraction while my three-year-old stared at me, his glittery $5,000 wedge reflecting in the beads of sweat on my forehead amid the Houston humidity.

Our second son, Grayson Matthew, joined our family on November 1, 2010, in what was the exact opposite of my first birth experience. I arrived at the hospital after laboring at home, monitor free, and a short two hours later, I had a successful, unmedicated vaginal birth after cesarean (VBAC). My body was finally able to do what God intended it to do: deliver life in its own time.

Grayson and I immediately had skin-to-skin bonding. I will never forget the awe and wonder of watching my minutes-old son scoot and push with his beautiful, nonparalyzed legs up my torso, latch on to my breast, and begin nursing with his fully functioning suck/swallow/breathe coordination. I had never seen such a wonder in all my life. What a far cry this was from my first delivery in a sterile operating room, where my ill son had been whisked away from me. This was a redemptive, beautiful moment God had given me.

As all became stable, my husband and I were transferred to a postpartum room *with our baby*. What a treat! As we settled into our room, the unit's admitting nurse asked, "So this is your second son? How exciting!" Assuming we were old pros, she left us ... alone! With a newborn! We had no clue how to burp an hours-old baby or how to properly swaddle a tiny child free of any tubes and wires. I had no idea how to nurse a child (although I could operate a Medela hospital-grade breast pump in my sleep!).

In that instant, I realized we were brand-new parents. Again. Everything we knew about infants was for medically fragile babies. Our learning curve was going to be steep for this second-firstborn son of ours. We had no idea what milestones to watch for, like when to introduce solid food, when to expect him to sit up or crawl or walk, and we might hear his first word. This was going to be another great adventure for us.

Though adding another child to our family was a wonderful blessing, it was also exhausting and challenging. My parents lived four hours away, Ryan's, six hours. And we needed them desperately. Private duty nursing coverage for Hayden had always been hit or miss, depending on the season, which historically had been just another opportunity for us to go with the flow. It wasn't as easy, however, to serve as a private duty nurse while also caring for a newborn.

During one particular "shift" as Hayden's nurse, I also served as the nurse for Grayson. Hayden was on his play mat on the floor, and his oxygen levels began to drop. The monitor alarmed, letting me know he needed to be suctioned. Grayson was cuddled up with me on the couch, eating his second breakfast (or third or fourth?—they all became a blur.) At that moment, and all the ones to ever follow,

Hayden won. I had to help him, no matter the cost. So with a baby on my breast, I left the cozy cuddling couch and carried him with me to the mat, where I laid him down so I could suction Hayden. Being in two places at one time is never an easy task—a lesson I'm still having confirmed to me on a daily basis.

Ryan and I prayed for an opportunity to move closer to our families. We would've loved the chance to raise our kids in a small town, but access to a pediatric hospital was our top priority. God soon blessed us with a job opportunity for Ryan that moved us from Houston to Dallas. This move set us nearly dead center between our two families in East and West Texas, which cut our travel times to the grandparents in half!

We found ourselves on another adventure, moving into a rental house—sight unseen—in the suburbs of Dallas. But we had learned by now that accommodations aren't what make up a family; it's the members of the family that make us who we are. We are more than our address.

One spring day in 2011, with a five-month-old baby and a four-year-old packed into our SUV towing a small trailer with bare essentials, we headed out for a brand-new journey, our hearts full of hope, our eyes wide with excitement, and our palms open to whatever God was going to show us in this new place.

∞

Settling into our new routine in a new city took a bit longer than it probably would have for a typical family since we had to start from the ground up with establishing care for Hayden's new medical team. It took a while, but eventually we figured out the medical system and felt established. God had been so kind to place us closer to our families and to give us doctors and nurses who could help us with Hayden's numerous medical needs.

A year into our new life, when the boys were two and five, we began to ponder what it would be like if we expanded our family again. This time, to my surprise, it was my idea. After some discussion, Ryan and I agreed to try for three kids, but we felt the time was not right yet. Grayson was only two, and even though Hayden was attending kindergarten, he still required a lot of therapies and weekly appointments. In an attempt to make a wise decision (or more than likely, in an effort to be in control of our circumstances), we decided to circle back to this dream in the future and not move forward with another baby at that time.

Have you ever had a surprise party thrown for you? I think you can see where this story goes. God gave us quite the surprise when only weeks later we found out I was pregnant. An epic reminder of who is actually before all things and in whom "all things hold together" (Colossians 1:17).

∽

In the previous chapter, we learned a lot from Job and his experience of loss and grief. But do you know how things ended for Job? Way better than they started, that's for certain. Job 42:10 (MSB) tells us, "After Job had prayed for his friends, the LORD restored his prosperity and doubled his former possessions." *Doubled!* Verse 12 (MSB) says, "So the LORD blessed Job's latter days more than his first." Job was resilient and unwavering in his trust of God, even when all of his expectations in life went unmet. And in His kindness, God restored Job.

We've all had expectations go unmet. Twists and turns in life that we did not see coming, surprises—both good and bad—that shocked us to our core. In February 2013, in His kindness, just as He did for Job, God restored and doubled to me the loss I had experienced from Hayden's birth. Our third son, Ethan Judson, was the best surprise I never knew I needed. Though his pregnancy was unplanned, it certainly wasn't unwanted.

We quickly overcame the shock and eagerly awaited our latest gift. I was reminded of that word I had received from the Lord: *Whatever child you get is for My glory, not yours.* We were excited to see what God would do with the life of this child He had given us.

God granted me a second unmedicated VBAC and another positive birth experience of bonding, health, and happiness, free of neonatologists, infant IVs, and empty postpartum rooms. With our three sons, aged five and under, we settled into a new routine. "Staying alive" was our one and only goal for that season.

Watching how God cared for our family and sustained our physical needs made me all the more aware of His love for me. In the times when I didn't even know what I needed, God was working and moving behind the scenes. From job changes to statewide moves to gifting us with three wonderful sons, God never left us. He always had a divine plan, even when we couldn't see it.

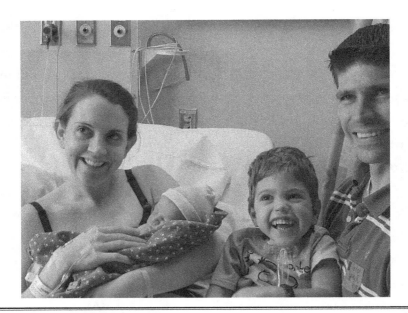

Family of four when Grayson is born, November 1, 2010, in Houston, Texas

Mom and Dad outnumbered when Ethan is born, February 21, 2013, in Plano, Texas

CHAPTER NINE

Know for Yourself

*God's love has been poured into our hearts through
the Holy Spirit who has been given to us.*

ROMANS 5:5

Our brains are incredible organs, aren't they? Designed so intricately by God to keep us alive, breathing and thinking, functioning and feeling. There's so much that scientists and doctors don't know about the brain. During Hayden's extensive surgery on his abdomen when he was in the NICU, the pediatric surgeon told me the "belly and the brain are still both black boxes" for doctors. Even professionals can't understand all the intricacies of this organ.

Are you familiar with the Mandela Effect? It's the idea of a false memory, when someone recalls something that didn't actually happen. For example, many people quote the famous line from *Star Wars*, "Luke, I am your father." Except the quote is actually, "No, I am your father."[8] But we've heard it the first way so many times, we just accept and believe it.

There's another phenomenon called an *information cascade* in which people follow trends or behaviors based on what they've seen other people doing, but not necessarily based on their own preference. Fashion trends are an example of this. The style we aim to achieve is set for us by executives in Paris and New York, and we simply assimilate, even if we secretly think it's tacky, because looking cool is more important than how we truly feel about the trend.

I'm intrigued by the way our brains function and how human behavior reflects the manner in which our brains work. I wonder if sometimes, especially when it comes to spiritual matters, we let our brains take a breather and put them on autopilot. I speculate that if we're honest, we can admit that it's easier to build our theology through the Mandela Effect or in an information cascade than through our own reading and studying of God's Word.

I grew up in the church, but I confess it wasn't until my early thirties that I read the entire Bible. Oh, I had read the Bible and had even gone through seasons of having consistent quiet devotion times, applying the parts of the Word I liked or understood to my own life. But I had never taken the time to read the entire metanarrative of God's Word.

Maybe you're like I was. You've been exposed to the Word, you've implemented parts of it, but you've never read the entire book in context. Statistics tell us that most believers are in the same boat.

One study reported that out of more than two billion Christians in the world, less than 30 percent will ever read through the entire Bible.[9] The vast majority of us (over 82 percent) only read their Bibles on Sundays during church services. On any given day, evangelicals in the US are twice as likely to use Facebook as they are to access their Bible. What is happening?[10]

Google's English Dictionary defines an "evangelical" as living "of or according to the teaching of the gospel or the Christian religion."[11] How can we live according to teachings we don't even know or haven't read for ourselves? If we want to look more like Christ, something has to change.

∾

In 2017, with life going pretty smoothly, God began stirring in my heart through a shift in our family's circumstances. Hayden had just turned ten, and his health had been decently stable, with only a couple of hospital visits per year for acute illnesses and surgeries. Grayson and Ethan, who were seven and three, were used to having nurses in our home, accompanying Hayden to doctor appointments and therapy visits, and the occasional shuffling to family and friends' homes for overnight stays during Hayden's emergency hospitalizations. The boys had nothing else to compare life to, and neither did Ryan and I. We were just living out our normal reality.

But a time came when we had to make difficult decisions regarding a planned major surgery for Hayden with a specialty team of surgeons out of state. Making the choice to risk a major, complicated procedure in hopes of an improved quality of life for Hayden put my faith to the test. In the midst of my making this decision, God drew me closer to Him and His Word. I began to enjoy studying Scripture more than I ever had. I became interested in eschatology, the study of the end times. Ryan and I hosted a small home group with fellow believers that occasionally met at our house. We began to sense God drawing us closer to Him and deeper into the Word.

With clarity, we chose to move forward with the medical procedure. Hayden's surgery took place in October 2017. It was the most difficult operation he had ever had to endure. (At the date of this publication, Hayden has had thirty-two surgeries.)

His recovery was terrible. As his sole caregiver, I had to stay in another Ronald McDonald House, this time in Ohio, for weeks. I felt pretty low. Thankfully, it's when we're at our lowest point that God is closest to us. The Word says, "The LORD is near to the brokenhearted" (Psalm 34:18). And that's what I was: brokenhearted. I was losing hope that Hayden would survive the recovery. Yet my faith grew deeper in trusting God's sovereign plan for my oldest son's life. Having spent the better part of the year digging into the Bible, I had gotten to know God deeply, and I knew I could trust Him in the uncertainty of Hayden's health.

Hayden required a second emergency surgery six weeks after the initial procedure, but he did finally recover. I was thankful God had been with me through it all and brought him out alive. The surgeries improved Hayden's independence and quality of life. However, following a two-month hospital stay, we lost all home nursing care for four months. It was quite a challenge, after spending months out of state as his sole caregiver, to come home and serve for another extended period of time as his nurse, while also performing all the homemaking and motherly duties for my other kids.

It took a toll on me physically and emotionally. The resignation of our home health nurse broke my heart, my body was beyond exhausted, and I felt invisible. But in these moments of complete desperation I drew even closer to God through His Word.

In Matthew 11, Jesus promised an easy yoke. My earthly yoke was incredibly heavy. In my humanity, I was dehydrated and thirsty. Yet God's Word reminded me daily that if I would come to Him, I "will never be thirsty again" (John 4:14). The Word of God is that powerful! It's a living, breathing love letter from our Father. The importance of reading it daily had already become evident to me. But the *how* of reading was an exciting new journey I was about to discover.

I see incredible value and beauty in the Old Testament. During my first trip through the Bible, I came to understand God as my good, good heavenly Father. Some people only see Jesus in the New Testament, but He is on every single page of the Old Testament too. He *is* the Word. He was present at creation, and He is present in countless theophanies and Christophanies, appearing to people before He became human Himself. If we fail to study the entire Bible and choose only the "parts with Jesus," we'll miss seeing all of God's character on display, unable to view and enjoy the entire metanarrative.

The Bible is *one* story of God's creation of people made to live in fellowship with Him, their sin and fall causing separation from Him, His plan to use His Son, Jesus, to rescue His people through His death and resurrection, and how one day, He will gather His followers to be reunited with Him in eternity, restoring fellowship with Him.

To help us understand the importance of reading the Bible for ourselves, I would like to introduce you to a New Testament character from the book of Acts, covering a time when the church as we know it was in its infancy. Following Jesus's death and resurrection, He spent forty days on earth before ascending to heaven (where He will reign until His second return, an event we eagerly anticipate). Jesus spent these few weeks with His followers and disciples, offering more instructions on how to love and care for people after He was gone and how to spread the gospel. He told them, "Go therefore and make disciples of all the nations, baptizing them in the name of the Father and of the Son and of the Holy Spirit" (Matthew 28:19 NKJV). And that's what His followers did after they received the Holy Spirit at Pentecost, when the church was born.

The writer of Acts describes the birth of the church, the coming of the Holy Spirit, the death of the first martyr for the gospel, and Saul's conversion to Christianity and his subsequent name change to Paul. Then we see the gospel spread through all nations, just as Jesus instructed. In chapter 8, one of Jesus's disciples, Philip, heeds the prompting of an angel of the Lord who tells him to head to a particular spot of the road near Gaza in a desert area. The text tells us, "And he rose and went" (Acts 8:27). There's an entire sermon in that sentence about being in tune with the Lord's prompting and heeding instructions given to us by the Spirit that we just get up and obey. But we'll put a pin in that lesson for now.

When Philip arrives at the meeting spot, per the angelic instructions he had received, he comes across a man in a chariot on his way back home to Ethiopia. This man, a eunuch and court official of the queen of Ethiopia, had been in Jerusalem to worship. Some commentaries note that in ancient times, the term *eunuch* was oftentimes synonymous with *treasurer*, so it's possible this term is just letting the reader understand this man's high position on the queen of Ethiopia's administration team.[12]

This gentleman had been in worship and was now riding in his chariot, heading home. Philip overheard him reading out loud from the book of Isaiah. Another prompting from the Spirit told Philip he needed to hop into the chariot and check on the eunuch. Philip ran to him and asked him, "Do you understand what you are reading?" (Acts 8:30). Kudos to Philip, yet again, for doing exactly what the Spirit told him to do and for talking to a stranger. Neither of those things comes very easy to me.

The eunuch answered Philip's question with a question. "How can I, unless someone guides me?" (Acts 8:31). The eunuch invited Philip to take a seat and talk Scripture with him. This man was worshiping and seeking, reading the Word for himself, and was hungry for knowledge and to be discipled, but he wasn't sure where to begin. God honored that behind the scenes. His Spirit was working, prompting, and moving people and circumstances just perfectly so that this holy encounter could take place.

The passage the eunuch had been reading aloud was from Isaiah 53, known in the modern day as the "forbidden chapter" because this portion of Scripture is omitted from most Jewish synagogues.[13] The verses say, "Like a sheep he was led to the slaughter and like a lamb before its shearer is silent, so he opens not his mouth. In his humiliation justice was denied him. Who can describe his generation? For his life is taken away from the earth" (Acts 8:32–33).

This chapter of Isaiah from the Old Testament prophesied about Jesus. God told His people hundreds of years before Jesus arrived, clothed in humanity, what they should be on the lookout for. But the eunuch was unsure of who this text was referring to, and he asked Philip to clarify—were the verses describing Isaiah or someone else?

Understanding Scripture on our own can be quite challenging. For those of us living in the twenty-first century, in a culture that is nothing like the ancient world, we're out of context with the biblical text. Without seeing the full picture of this single metanarrative, it can feel incredibly confusing.

When I feel confused, I shut down. Maybe you lean toward digging in and studying harder. Or you might quit when you feel overwhelmed because that's the path of least resistance. But there's a fail-proof strategy to understanding Scripture. It starts with asking the Holy Spirit to help us understand it. It is possible to be "filled with the knowledge of his will in all spiritual wisdom and understanding." Otherwise, why would this be the prayer Paul prayed over the church in Colossae in Colossians 1:9?

Philip explains to the eunuch that this passage from Isaiah was actually describing Jesus, the Messiah, who had overcome death and ascended to heaven only days prior. The eunuch heard the gospel of Jesus, and he believed! He was seeking, the Spirit was moving, Philip was explaining, and lives were transformed.

As they continued on their way in the wagon, they came upon a body of water, and when he saw it, the eunuch asked Philip to baptize him right there and then. No need to wait until the next church service and coordinate family and a celebratory cake—he was ready to do the next step that Jesus had commanded His followers to do (Matthew 28:19).

I've told you before that the Bible is a quite the page-turner, full of wild stories.

Immediately following the baptism, Philip essentially "teleported" out of the river via the Holy Spirit and was taken to Azotus, another town where he preached the gospel (Acts 8:39–40). So the eunuch was left standing alone in the river, drenched, having just been raised to walk in the newness of life. And he rejoiced! He hopped back into his wagon and made his way to Ethiopia to live out the Great Commission. He returned to his hometown and his duties, but as he did, he fulfilled the prophecy that was spoken of in Matthew 28 when Jesus said the gospel would be spread to all the nations.

Christians are called to know the Scriptures and be equipped and ready to share the gospel. "Always be prepared to give an answer to everyone who asks you to give the reason for the hope that you have" (1 Peter 3:15 NIV). It's vital that we read God's Word for ourselves and don't rely on a weekly sermon as our only exposure to Scripture. We've got to be Bereans.

In Acts 17, when Paul and Silas were on one of their missionary journeys, they ran into a group of Jewish believers in Berea. These believers were considered to be of "more noble character" than others in the region because they "examined the Scriptures every day to see if what Paul said was true" (Acts 17:11 NIV).

Friends, that's what we all should be doing. Gone are the days when we can just sit under pastors or Bible study teachers and blindly believe their messages. It's time for us to know the Word for ourselves and examine the teachings we hear against what God Himself says to us in His Word.

Maybe you are on board with this plan, and you want to be equipped to study and examine God's Word, but you have no idea where to begin. That's where I was. Ready to become a Berean and learn the Scriptures for myself. And God was preparing me for a journey through His Word that would literally change everything.

∽

For Christmas 2019, I asked for a new Bible. I picked the English Standard Version because I had never owned that one before. On the first crisp, new page, little lines were provided to write on. I wrote, "2019. This is my year to read the entire Bible."

Days after writing those words, a friend texted me and asked if I'd like to try a Bible reading plan with her for the new year. Called "The Bible Recap," this was a chronological reading plan that would walk us through the entire Bible in 365 days. After each day's portion of Bible reading, we would listen to a brief podcast hosted by Tara-Leigh Cobble that would summarize that day's passage. This sounded perfect! I invited a couple of other girlfriends to join in on this plan as well.

Reading in community with friends was just what I needed to take my first trip through the entire Bible. And boy, did this plan change everything for me! If you need a plan to take your inaugural trek through all of the Bible, I cannot recommend The Bible Recap enough.[14]

During the completion of this Bible reading plan, I fell deeply in love with God's Word. Most mornings, before my house came to life, I listened to the Bible app on my phone while following along in my new hard-copy Bible. I journaled notes and tidbits that God opened my eyes to, things I had never seen before. Those were my favorite moments—in the quiet and stillness, cozied up in the corner of my bedroom with coffee, a Bible, and my favorite Flair pens.

Of course, there were some days when life got busy, but I still listened to the day's passage and the podcast, oftentimes in my car on the way to the school pickup or drop-off line. Much like the Ethiopian eunuch, I spent time during my commute to dig into the Word. I prayed and sought wisdom to understand Scripture, and God was faithful to answer that prayer.

Learning information and facts about the Bible is great. But a change in our hearts and behavior is really what we seek when we draw close to the Lord and get to know Him through His Word. During my first trip through Scripture, I learned of God's heart for the oppressed, for the poor and widows, the orphans, and foreigners. Soon that knowledge led to my own heart change. And as my heart changed, so did my entire family.

CHAPTER TEN

A Storm Rolls In

Just because something is hard it doesn't mean it's bad.
It just means it's hard.

—JAMIE IVEY

I love to read. A poster in one of the classrooms I attended during my years of public education read, "Good readers make great writers." (Gosh I hope that's true!) In 2019, with my fresh Bible becoming increasingly highlighted and marked up, I began to explore a few other books that somehow ended up in my hands (read: "God put them in front of me").

Most readers have lists of their all-time favorite books. I bet you could rattle off a couple of titles that come to mind if I asked you which books changed your life. *Radical* by David Platt, published in 2010, messed me up in the best way. Platt speaks and writes in an honest way that essentially calls out super-obvious actions that churches and Christians do (or *don't* do) and compares those things to Christ. He goes through all sorts of topics, from his church's snack budget for goldfish crackers to our culture's obsession with the American dream.

One topic Platt wrote about was the idea of being pro-life. After being pro-life for my entire life even serving as a volunteer at a crisis pregnancy center after college, I wrestled with living out my convictions for a split second when I was offered a termination treatment plan for Hayden. Watching God use his life to change so much about my world and the lives of countless others has made me even more steadfast in my conviction that every life is precious and created by God for a purpose.

My first complete trip through the Bible in 2019 confirmed that to me, as every chapter revealed to me more of God's character and heart.

I know we don't all subscribe to the exact same theology, and that's okay; we can still be friends. But I highly recommend all Christians who are actively seeking to look more like Christ as they live out their faith to check out *Radical* and see if you recognize yourself on any of the pages. That's where I found myself, for better or worse.

David Platt tells his readers that we cannot be pro-life and do nothing. Until that sentence, I had never heard a pastor or biblical teacher come right out and say what needed to be said. Having convictions is one thing; living out those convictions is a whole other ball game.

If I said that pink is my favorite color, but I had no pink items in my wardrobe, water bottles, key chains, pens, phone case, home decor, or hand towels, that would be weird, right? I mean, if pink is my favorite color, wouldn't it show up in some of the items I use daily? If I tell you I'm pro-life, but you don't see evidence of that in my life, am I *really* pro-life?

Caveat here: sometimes others can't see the private works you're doing, like anonymous donations or providing help to a single mom or having dinner delivered monthly to a homeless shelter. It's not about the works you're doing, but you know in your heart of hearts where you stand on this issue.

Our works do not save us. Only faith in Jesus Christ as our Savior does that. We are completely free in Him, and we don't have to *do* anything to earn our salvation. "For by grace you have been saved through faith. And this is not your own doing; it is the gift of God, not a result of works, so that no one may boast" (Ephesians 2:8–9). By laying down our lives with an outpouring of His love in us, we seek to serve those around us. As our hearts are transformed to be more and more like His, the way we spend our time, how we use our money, the thoughts we have—these all begin to change.

The year I completed The Bible Recap reading plan and podcasts, my entire life changed. It recalibrated my understanding of who God is and how He feels about me, and consequently, the way I lived my life began to change.

⤨

When Ryan and I began to ponder the idea of whether a person could be pro-life and do nothing, we went to Scripture. I had been reading daily about God's heart for the orphan and the widow, the sojourner and the oppressed. It seemed like, for the first time in my life, I was realizing that much of the rhetoric I had heard in the church (not strictly from the pulpit, but from professing Christ followers) was perhaps not completely in line with Scripture after all.

The message from my religious community, as I had interpreted it, was that people who had fallen into struggles due to their life choices (drug addiction, children out of wedlock with multiple people, systemic poverty) should just make better choices. Stop doing drugs. Get married to one person and then start a family. Persevere for a job option with better pay. Yet I was reading over and over again of a God who not only loved *all* people in *all* circumstances, but He was also frequently put out with His people (the Israelites) for oftentimes turning their backs on the "poor and needy" (Ezekiel 16:49).

Before my salvation in Jesus, I was an orphan with no hope and no heavenly Father. But through Christ's sacrifice, I had been made a child of God, adopted into His family, and given a "wonderful inheritance" (Psalm 16:6 NLT). His promise was true that He would not leave me as an orphan but that He would come to me (John 14:18).

Coming to understand this dichotomy of what I had always heard and what I was actively discovering for myself left me standing in the middle of a crossroads. Knowing and believing God is who He says He is and learning about His heart and compassion for the vulnerable, Ryan and I prayed about what that meant for our lives. We evaluated passages of Scripture like James 1:27, where we learned that "religion that is pure and undefiled before God the Father is this: to visit orphans and widows in their affliction, and to keep oneself unstained from the world." We wondered what that would mean in this day and age.

We attended an informational meeting with a foster agency to learn about what needs they had and see if we could be of any help to them. Buckner International is a Christian agency that has been around since 1879 and has an excellent track record, and it was a great place to start. During that initial meeting, we learned that respite care was an ongoing need of foster agencies. Short-term care (fourteen days or fewer) to children in foster care gives full-time foster parents a short break from caring for the child, or the opportunity to travel out of state since foster children can't easily cross state lines, if they had booked a vacation and didn't know to include the new foster child in the ticket purchase.

This seemed like the perfect spot to dip our toes into foster care. We had begun to live our lives by something we heard Pastor Francis Chan say: to walk in a yes until it's a no in response to commands God has explicitly given us in Scripture. I knew God's instructions when it came to helping orphans, widows, and the vulnerable. Clearly, doing something to help was a definite yes.

Narrowing down God's specific will for our family as to exactly *how* was up for debate. It seemed He was leading us to move forward with the Buckner agency, so we took steps toward yes. Each informational session, each interview with Buckner staff, and each class we attended was one more yes. We walked into the process with openness, knowing that at any moment, they could tell us we weren't a good fit and our yes could become a no. We were comfortable with that as we took baby steps of faith.

Each class we attended was an opportunity to walk faithfully in trust of God's plan for us and also a way for our marriage to become a ministry. Foster care was something Ryan and I were completely united about, but, overwhelmingly, this is not typically the case. I've talked to many wives who told me they would love to foster but their husbands aren't on board. That makes me a little sad, of course, but it also makes me incredibly grateful that Ryan has always led our family well in our foster care journey. He has been an invested co-laborer in what God has called us to as a couple.

Back when *zoom* was just the noise a fast car made, and no one knew what a virtual meeting was, we had meetings in person. (Remember those days?) The initial classes to become licensed foster parents through Buckner were held on the agency's campus, forty-five minutes from our home. Once a week for six weeks, we secured a nurse to watch Hayden and a babysitter to watch Grayson and Ethan, and we made the trek through Dallas evening traffic to attend the classes. Each week our attendance became one more yes from God.

Providing respite care requires a foster license by the state, just like full-time foster parenting. During these weeks of babysitters and being shuffled around, our kids came to understand the important role they played in our family becoming licensed. We talked with them about our decision every step of the way, and none of them ever hesitated to move forward. We were intentional in explaining that when they cooperated with the babysitter, they were playing a role in the licensing process—they were losing hours weekly with their mom and dad so that our family could become equipped to help a child who didn't have a mom and dad able to care for them.

Our entire process to become licensed was on the lengthy side due to our busy schedules and all the training hours and paperwork. At a snail's pace, we continued to walk in yeses. After ten months, we became an officially licensed foster home, available to provide respite care to full-time foster parents. With eager anticipation and a healthy amount of nerves, we hung our foster license on the wall (per state protocol) and waited to see who God would bring through our doors.

∽

When you become foster parents, you are asked about your placement preferences for ages, needs, races, religions, etc. Due to the ages of our children, we figured a three-year-old or younger child would be the best fit in keeping with our established birth order. Our preference was for a boy since we already had three of them; we knew all about boys and had enough Hot Wheels and LEGO blocks to open a daycare center.

We had a couple of respite placements of young boys, and I felt proud of my three sons for their welcoming and helpful attitudes during those first initial cases. There's always a bit of nervousness when you're about to invite a stranger to stay in your home. You hope they like you, you hope they feel welcomed and at home, and you hope they get along okay with everyone. Our agency was wonderful and helped make those first few cases smooth and easy transitions.

One morning, six months after becoming licensed, I got a call from our agency. The staff member on the phone asked if we could provide up to two weeks of respite care for a foster child whose foster parent was going to have a medical procedure and wouldn't be able to lift the child. I checked my calendar and saw that one of the two weeks would include spring break, but with no travel plans set, we were available. I asked for the boy's name and for details about his case. To my surprise, they were calling about a girl. I got the details of this sweet little two-year-old and thought to myself, *You can do anything for two weeks.*

Girls made Ryan and me nervous simply because we had no experience with them. What do girls like to do? Would she mind playing in the dirt with our bunch of rowdy boys? How do you fix a girl's hair? Even with all these unknowns, the only thing to do was say yes and keep walking in it until it was a no.

In March 2019, a curly-haired toddler named Stormy was dropped off at our house by her foster mother. Stormy was shy and timid and had a suitcase full of clothes and an arm full of baby dolls.

She spoke a few words and sentences at first but began to open up a day or two after being with us.

Five days into her two-week stay with us, I went into my bathroom, and on the other side of the door I heard a little voice saying, "Mommy?" I was flattered that this little girl was calling me Mommy and excited to know I had gained her trust. (Of course, that's what three other kids in the home called me, so it came naturally to her to do the same.)

We had a lovely two weeks with Stormy. My boys adored her and doted on her. We took her to church and to restaurants with us. Ryan's parents got to meet her when they came to town. She seemed to fall right into place as a member of our family.

And then, our two weeks were up. A respite case can't last more than fourteen days, and the day came when Stormy had to return to her foster home.

On Sunday after church, we left our boys with Ryan's parents, and Ryan and I drove Stormy to her original foster home, forty-five minutes from us. She started to cry as soon as we pulled up to the house. It made me so sad. She clung to me and cried for me. Transitions are always hard for little kids, but even more so for children who have been through significant trauma.

Ryan and I went into the house with her and visited with the foster parents and their biological son. We tried our best to make the transition back into the home as smooth as possible for Stormy's sake. But I was in tears alongside the other foster mom and Stormy.

In the foster classes everything we learned was all theory. Living out this sadness was gut-wrenching. And if *I* was taking it this hard, how was this innocent child processing all of the hurt and shuffling she'd endured in her two short years?

Our drive home was quiet, full of sadness and mourning. Ryan's parents were just as sad to see Stormy go as we were. When they said goodbye through tears and made their way back to West Texas, I grieved in the peaceful calm of our home, now absent of a two-year-old. The evening was solemn and still, until a dark cloud moved in and a giant spring thunderstorm popped up. It felt like God was affirming that He saw us in our sadness and had brought a rain storm to hover over us and remind us of little Stormy, who had made a lasting impression on our family in such a short time. Watching through tears as the rain fell that Sunday afternoon, I knew Stormy would always have a place in my heart. What I didn't know was that soon my home would hold her as well.

CHAPTER ELEVEN

Bravely Reckless

Character produces hope, and hope does not put us to shame.

ROMANS 5:4–5

I don't wear glasses. My vision is fine, for now, although I'm aging more quickly with each passing day, so I know my time is coming. However, I do use "Bible glasses." I view the world and everything around me through the lens of Scripture. I have a biblical worldview.

When counseling my kids through current world events, I always start by stating the facts, then immediately I ask them to put their Bible glasses on and consider what Scripture says about the topic at hand. If we can't find the answer explicitly (e.g., "What age does the Bible say is appropriate to give your child a cell phone?"), we think about God's character. Based on what we know about God, we consider what behavior, choice, or action would bring God the most glory, and we move forward from there.

We tend to view the world through the lens of the setting we grew up in. Maybe you come from a family of farmers, and waking up early every morning to tackle farm chores was the baseline, and it wasn't until you left for college that you realized not everyone in the world is up at 4:00 a.m. to milk cows.

I'm a fourth-generation East Texan from the Piney Woods, and I love trees. I didn't grasp the fact that I had grown up in an actual forest until the first time Ryan took me to his hometown in West Texas. On my inaugural trip to his tiny rural town, I was overly excited to see a real cactus. I also had genuine concerns about all the sad, tiny trees on his parents' property. (Turns out they were mesquite trees. They weren't dying; they were just small compared to the beautiful, tall pine trees I was used to seeing behind the Pine Curtain of East Texas.)

Though I love trees, I'm no arborist. We have a tree in our backyard that has never made sense to me. When we moved in, we were told it was a pear tree. Every year we wondered if this would be the year it was going to produce fruit, what with it being a pear tree and all. Until we realized it's called a fruitless pear tree—*Pyrus calleryana*, to be scientific. This tree "offers the beauty of showy blooms and fall color, without the hassle of fruit production."[15] I also learned that this tree that bears no fruit is shallow-rooted and tolerates most soil types. (Maybe there's hope for me to become an arborist after all—just listen to all the tree facts I've learned!)

This fruitless fruit tree, while wearing my Bible glasses, reminds me of what we as Christians are called to do. The Bible was written at a time when agriculture was key to human survival, so it shouldn't surprise us that many of the applications and illustrations in the text are based on farming and agriculture.

Bearing fruit is highly encouraged in the Bible. Jesus tells us in John 15 that He, Himself, is the vine and we are the branches. Jesus (as the vine) feeds us (His followers), and the gardener (the Father) tends to and prunes the branches. John 15:2 further details this beautiful analogy: "Every branch in me that does not bear fruit he takes away, and every branch that does bear fruit he prunes, that it may bear more fruit."

What does it mean to bear fruit? First, it means that we, as followers of Christ, are reflecting Jesus's character. If we don't look like the vine, we aren't reflecting our source of life. Our attitudes, our hearts, and our demeanor toward those around us should be Christlike, not self-serving. Our outward actions are evidence of our inward hearts.

The fruit we bear as followers of Jesus should benefit other people, not just us. When we look like Christ, we lay down our lives and humbly put others above ourselves.

⌒⌒⌒⌒

Before we had the New Testament example of the vine and the vinedresser, we had the Old Testament example given to us by Isaiah. The prophet described Israel as the Lord's vineyard. "God expected His vineyard to bear fruit, but it produced nothing but worthless grapes"[16] (Isaiah 5:1–7). Even in the Old Testament, God was seeking followers who would bear fruit, selflessly living for others and visibly displaying an inward heart of trust in Him. We meet someone like that in the book of Esther.

Esther is one of only two books in the Bible where the name of God is not mentioned, yet He is clearly on every page of the story, working providentially behind the scenes for the sake of His people and in the life of a particular Jewish woman.

Esther was an orphan being raised by her cousin, Mordecai. Through a crazy set of circumstances including a king's wild party and a queen who wasn't in the mood for shenanigans, a job opening came up for a new queen in the kingdom. An odd type of beauty pageant began, and Esther found herself in the running to fill the vacancy. She heeded Mordecai's advice and kept her heritage a secret. And in God's providence, Esther was selected as the "winner."

Serving in her new role, Esther lived in the palace but rarely saw the king. In fact, beyond her beauty, there doesn't appear to be much the king knew about Esther. He didn't even realize she was Jewish.

Esther became aware of a plot formulating outside the walls of the kingdom in which Haman, an evil employee of the king, hoped to destroy Mordecai and all the Jews in the land. Haman drafted a letter, and had it sealed with the king's signet ring, which gave permission for the officials "to destroy, to kill, and to annihilate all Jews . . . and to plunder their goods" (Esther 3:13).

As she considered the looming reality of what was to come for herself and her fellow Jewish people, Esther had a difficult decision to make. Say nothing and fly under the radar as a hidden Jew? Or speak up and ask the king for help on behalf of her people? Even for the queen, it was unacceptable to go to the king without being summoned by him. Doing so could easily result in her immediate death.

This was Esther's chance to decide what type of fruit her tree was going to bear.

Her first step was to ask all the Jews in her hometown of Susa to fast on her behalf, and she would do the same. For three days they would not eat or drink but rather pray. Esther's fruit reflected someone who was dependent on God and who sought Him in prayer for wise counsel.

Esther told Mordecai her plan, and she ended her correspondence to him with this profound statement: "Then I will go to the king, though it is against the law, and if I perish, I perish" (Esther 4:16). When given the opportunity to risk her life and safety for the sake of countless Jews, Esther answered with a brave and reckless yes.

God had placed Esther in a circumstance "for such a time as this" (Esther 4:14), and she boldly walked forward, trusting in God's sovereignty over her life. She reflected God's character and His heart for His people, especially when they're vulnerable. Her actions of faith were visible to those around her in her three-day fast, and they were made visible to the king when she approached him, risking it all. And her attempt to keep an entire people group alive showed that Esther was willing to lay down her life for the sake of others.

Fear makes a terrible master. If the Spirit of the living God indwells you, He will not give you a spirit of fear (2 Timothy 1:7). Esther faced her fears head-on. She overcame her fear of the consequences of speaking to the king uninvited because the lives of the vulnerable meant more to her than her own self-preservation. And God honored her faith. When she approached the king, he graciously allowed her to speak her mind.

In a royal encounter between Esther, the king, and Haman, Esther boldly revealed to the king the evil plan Haman had set in motion. The appalled king, coming to her defense, ended Haman's life and had the decree edited so the Jewish people of the land were able to defend themselves against any threats against them.

The story ends with the Jews gaining "mastery over those who hated them" (Esther 9:1). In this, we see more of God's heart revealed. He brings good news, binds up the brokenhearted, proclaims liberty, frees prisoners, and comforts those who mourn (Isaiah 61:1–2). We also see how great the impact can be when we answer bravely with a yes, even when it seems reckless to others.

⁓

We're often faced with opportunities to visibly reveal our fruit, to show the world whose vine we are abiding in. Ask yourself right now, who needs your help? Who are you available to help but haven't stepped out in faith and done so yet? Where are there opportunities for you to grow deeper in your faith by answering God's call with a brave yes rather than timidly retreating on account of busyness or feeling unqualified?

If you are in Christ, He is doing a work in you. If you're not actively bearing fruit now, He's pruning you for the future fruit you will bear. Jesus said, "Every branch in me that does not bear fruit he takes away, and every branch that does bear fruit he prunes, that it may bear more fruit" (John 15:2).

In the book of Matthew, Jesus warned His followers to pay attention to what fruit someone bears. "Are grapes gathered from thornbushes, or figs from thistles? So, every healthy tree bears good fruit, but the diseased tree bears bad fruit. A healthy tree cannot bear bad fruit, nor can a diseased tree bear good fruit. . . . Thus you will recognize them by their fruits" (Matthew 7:16–18, 20).

Reading this verse makes me wonder, am I recognizable? Are you? Would those around you, in your workplace or in your neighborhood, notice something visible, selfless, and reflective of God's character in your behavior, your language, your choices?

The great news is that we are all a constant work in progress. This is what sanctification, being conformed to the image of Christ, looks like. It's knowing Jesus and being free in Him, but also being a work in progress. It's constantly growing and changing, being refined to look more and more like Christ each day until we are glorified in heaven. As we align ourselves with God and His character, the outward display of our faith grows more evident.

When our faith is rooted in Him, and we've built our house on the rock, as Matthew 7:24 says, we are firm and steady. From that place of steadiness we can boldly say yes to the ways God wants to use us to further His kingdom.

In following Christ, we won't be like the fruitless pear tree that is shallow-rooted and tolerates most soil types.[17] Rather, our goal is to have deep roots, planted by the Living Water, so when life's storms come, the rain falls, and the wind beats against us, we will not be moved. We will not fall to the temporal things of the world.

Let us keep our eyes on eternity and have our decisions informed by who we are in Christ.

God used Hayden's diagnosis and life challenges to shape me into someone more like Jesus. God loved me enough that when I was too selfish to lay down my life, He put me into a circumstance that forced me to do so. It was as if God knew that He had to help me lose my life for His sake so I could find it (Matthew 10:39). What a gift He gave to me!

Having an opportunity to learn how to lay down my life for someone else changed everything about who I am. Yes, all parents die to themselves with their children—getting up exhausted for those middle-of-the-night feedings, exchanging Saturday morning brunch dates with girlfriends for tying soccer cleats and hauling lawn chairs onto a grassy field, agreeing to yet another trip to a pizza buffet when what you really want is a sushi roll. The difference is, in typical circumstances, those things are outgrown. One day your healthy child will sleep through the night, and so will you. Eventually, they'll be done with Little League and will sleep in until noon on Saturdays and find ways to avoid you for the rest of the weekend. And one day they'll be gone, adulting, and you will get dibs on your dinner destination every night.

Not so for parents of children with certain disabilities. It was in this acknowledgment that I was changed completely. I've had to truly lay down my life every moment of every day. Is it exhausting? Yes, 100 percent. Am I called to do this? Yes.

Through the gift of the challenging circumstances of Hayden's life, I learned how to die to myself in other arenas too. I began to explore areas where I could serve and to look for more opportunities to die to self, allowing Christ to shape me even more into who He asks His followers to be.

I started making decisions based on that mindset. Was there a way I could help someone? Would I look more like Jesus by doing it? Could I do anything today that would serve another person? If all of those questions were answered with a yes, I moved forward—even knowing that to the world it would look reckless and maybe even stupid.

That's the thing about this upside-down kingdom. It doesn't look like the world. And I don't want to look like this broken world either. I want to look like Jesus, and I want to live for eternity.

Saying yes to big adventures of faith is what makes followers of Christ stand out from the crowd. Those of us who follow Jesus are *all* called to be outliers. Why would we want to fit in when we are called to stand out?

Without these crucial changes in my heart and mind, I never would have stepped into foster care and bravely accepted where God was leading me.

Given the wheelchair, handicap van, oxygen tanks, suction machines, and loud monitors we travel with at all times, our family was used to visibly looking different from the world. Going out in public meant all eyes were on us. But we have no shame in who we are and who Hayden is.

Our other sons have always been used to curious stares, never shrinking back and hiding, so Ryan and I embraced our differences even more. We came to understand that God was equipping us for an even wilder family dynamic that would attract even more attention from outsiders. There was going to be one more spotlight put on our family—another opportunity to bravely choose to use our light to reflect Jesus to the world.

CHAPTER TWELVE

Ride The Waves

Don't plan it all. Let life surprise you a little.

JULIA ALVAREZ

We are a beach-loving family, me more so than Ryan. (Sand sensory issues, anyone?) I love the calm, methodical way the waves crash onto the shore as I enjoy a beautiful sunset. And beachy waves come naturally to my thick head of hair.

In 2019, as the school year began to wind down, our family decided to book a trip to a resort in Gulf Shores, Alabama, rather than visit our local Texas beaches. The kids were working hard in school—we had a kindergartener, a second grader, and a sixth grader—and our first year of exclusively homeschooling three kids was winding down, so a beach vacation was well deserved for us all. We made a countdown calendar and eagerly anticipated the end of the school year and the first day of summer break.

Stormy was always on our minds, and Ryan and I often said to each other, "I wonder what Stormy's doing right now." We hadn't seen her since March, but I sent occasional texts to her foster mom to check on her.

As our homeschooling and chaotic life with three young boys was in full swing, we continued to keep ourselves available as an open foster care respite home, so it wasn't a surprise when I got a phone call from Buckner in May. However, the question the agency asked was quite a surprise.

Rather than our usual short-term respite care, the caseworker asked if we could take a full-time placement. Although this wasn't what we had initially intended when getting licensed, we did have the appropriate licensure to handle this assignment.

Why on earth would we even consider a full-time placement when we already had three wild, homeschooling boys (including Hayden, with all his medical needs and concerns)? This wasn't a random placement. It was Stormy! After nine months in her foster home, for a variety of reasons, the staff needed to move her to a new foster home. The agency knew how much we had bonded with Stormy during our short time together, and we were at the top of their list for potential placement options.

We talked it over as a family and decided this would be a *major* yes to walk in. If God had allowed us to be considered for such a task, we would trust Him in it.

After an afternoon of deliberation, I called the agency and said we would love to welcome Stormy into our home, but with one caveat. We were about to leave Texas for a beach vacation and would have to postpone her arrival date. With some logistical coordination, we worked out a way for Stormy to come to us full time the day after we returned from Gulf Shores.

Our beach vacation was wonderful! Ryan and I treasured our time with the boys even more knowing our life would take on a new dynamic once we returned home.

Full-time placements are a much bigger commitment than respite care. They require frequent visits with caseworkers from the state, attorneys, and, in many cases, biological family members. There's paperwork and charting. We were up for the challenge, but we weren't naïve. We knew there would be a steep learning curve.

On May 25, 2019, we signed the paperwork for our first foster placement. Foster care is a place of tension. It's the space between being happy and dearly loving a child but also realizing that if things go well, the child will be reunited with family and you will experience losing them.

I often hear from people who don't feel equipped to foster because they fear becoming too attached. Well, that's the idea—to attach to the child and show love and compassion, while also teaching this skill to the child. When foster children are placed with their forever family, be it a biological relative or an adoptive placement, the ultimate goal is that they will have the skills to form a secure attachment with the family.

The details of Stormy's case are not mine to tell. Maybe one day she'll write her own book and share her journey with the world. But I can say that upon her placement with us, Stormy had been in foster care for nine months and the most pressing focus was to solidify permanency. Through conversations with numerous people on Stormy's team, Ryan and I expressed our openness and desire to adopt Stormy if that became an option.

Three weeks after Stormy was placed with us, her case took some dramatic twists and turns. After signing a lot of paperwork, Stormy's placement with us became a pending adoption.

Our small steps of yeses took us into a courtroom full of family and friends on National Adoption Day, November 23, 2019. Eight months after our first meeting and six months since she moved into our home permanently, Stormy Michelle Hensley became an official member of our family. What a surreal moment, watching all the tiny steps of faith come to fruition and getting to see how God worked to provide a family to the fatherless.

We had a pink, frilly family celebration the afternoon of the adoption ceremony and then quickly settled into the six-month break period that our agency recommended foster/adoptive families utilize once an adoption closes. This time is dedicated to establishing a secure bond and attachment to the newest family member without distractions from other potential foster placements coming into the home.

We enjoyed the Thanksgiving and Christmas holidays as a family of six—especially sharing photos of Stormy on our Christmas cards. No more hiding her face in photos, because she was now officially a Hensley!

Moving into 2020, we discussed what our next move should be when the six-month period came to a close. These were big decisions to make. Would we remain open to providing respite care? Or close our home and accept that our four kids would complete our family and conclude our season of serving in the foster space?

Little did we know that the feelings of uncertainty we experienced were soon to be felt by the entire world. March 2020 would bring big surprises to everyone. For our family, a couple of extra surprises were waiting in the wings.

∽∞∽

I once accompanied Ryan to a surfing lesson. By "accompanied," I mean I sat on the beach and watched him and his instructor in their matching wetsuits, sending videos to his parents, bragging about (and, to be honest, making fun of) his skills as a novice surfer-dude.

Experienced surfers stand comfortably on their boards, balancing with grace. In his lesson, Ryan learned how to lie on the board and watch for the right wave. When a good one was in his sights, he would move from a prone position and attempt to stand on his board to tackle the wave.

Unlike water sports that use an oar, surfing only works when there's a wave to ride. On a paddleboard or canoe, you can steer yourself any direction you choose. But for the adventure seeker, that would be much less risky and, consequently, less fun than trusting a wave, while standing solo on a board and finding the perfect balance of trust and skill.

At some point, floating on your stomach on the surfboard isn't enough. To make the most of the experience, you have to take a risk, stand up, strike the right balance, and go all in. If not for the power of the wave, you would be stagnant in the water—technically still floating but getting nowhere and missing the adrenaline rush.

Charles Spurgeon said, "I have learned to kiss the waves that throw me against the Rock of Ages."[18] Our family's wave was on its way. We were about to stand up and attempt our most difficult balancing act to date, trusting the Wave through it all.

Two months into the COVID-19 pandemic, we decided that with appropriate health and safety modifications, we would still be able to travel to our favorite Alabama beach to celebrate the end of the school year. Stormy would be able to take her first steps into the sand and experience the ocean. The trip felt like the perfect way to celebrate six months of Stormy being an official family member. We were thrilled to cross state lines with her without permission—one of the simple joys of moving from foster care to adoption.

Our days at the beach were restful and fun, spent making new memories as a family of six, playing games in our condo, making sand castles, even enjoying a surprise rain storm.

All too soon, the day came for us to load up and begin our drive home to Texas. As we waited for Ryan to finish loading our medical supplies and luggage into every nook and cranny of our wheelchair-converted van, the kids and I discussed how soon we would need to get serious about shopping for a bigger van. We decided to pray for direction from God about what van to look for. (I think the kids just prayed for one with a DVD player and an extra row of seats.)

We decided to break up the drive into two days, stopping in East Texas for the night to visit my parents. Along the way, Ryan and I brainstormed places we'd like to travel to as a couple. Family vacations tend to do that, don't they? They make you want to take an actual vacation—one without kids.

As we drove down a bumpy Louisiana back road, with our beach chairs shaking sand into our trunk with each pothole, my phone rang. Buckner was on the line. It had been a full six months since Stormy's adoption. Assuming they had called to ask whether we would be keeping our home open or not, I was shocked to find out the real reason for their call. Stormy had just become a big sister!

Our closed adoption meant we had no contact with Stormy's biological family. This phone call was one of, if not *the,* biggest surprises I had ever received. Without open communication with Stormy's bio family, we had no idea that her mother was pregnant.

In Texas, when a child enters foster care, it's protocol to first locate any biological siblings who are either in care or have been adopted in hopes of placing the children together. Since we were raising this new baby's closest relative, our agency offered this placement to us before looking for another foster home.

The news of Stormy having a biological sibling was shocking, but that shock went into overdrive when I heard, "Also, it's twins!"

"The boys just left the NICU and have nowhere to go tonight. You can have some time to think about it, but give us a call back soon and let us know if you would be willing to accept this placement."

Just moments before that phone call, our biggest worry was how soon we could get the van to a carwash and vacuum out the sand. Now we were contemplating a major, life-altering question. Would we say our biggest yes to date and give these three siblings whatever amount of time together this placement would allow? Or would we say no, close our home, ride off into the sunset, and go on that married-couple-only vacation we'd just been dreaming about?

Some decisions, like Esther's, require fasting and prayer for direction, while others only need one look from your partner, and you just know.

Ninety seconds later, I was on the phone agreeing to be the foster family to six-day-old twins. That is what foster care is—standing in the gap, taking an emergency placement, knowing your possible inconvenience is *nothing* compared to the trauma of being an infant with no home and no one to hold you. We wanted to be there for these babies but also for Stormy. These were her half-brothers, and we needed to give her every chance to spend as much time as possible with them before, or if, they went to back to family.

I called my neighbor Sarah and asked her to rally the troops in our neighborhood, raid attics and hand-me-downs, and see if we could drum up a couple of portable cribs, newborn clothes, and baby gear. While she went to work gathering supplies and cleaning my house, Ryan and I continued our drive home to Texas.

I hadn't had a baby in seven years, let alone two. Feeling a bit clueless about what I would need, I searched on Google "What does a newborn need?" I put together a pickup order at my local Walmart. As the miles home ticked down, the items in my online shopping cart piled up, and I hoped all those motherly instincts would soon kick in again.

At home, life became a blur. I didn't have time to critique my parenting skills. These beautiful, brown-skinned baby boys had us wrapped around their tiny fingers the minute we laid eyes on them. In this holy moment, as they lay in their borrowed beds on that first night in our home, wearing white NICU onesies, their only possessions in this world were the contents of a plastic hospital bag CPS dropped off with them—a comb, a nasal aspirator, and a hat knitted by hospital volunteers—I realized it was an incredible gift to even be considered to step in and help these precious babies. I got to love them, feed them, cuddle them, and teach them how much God loves them and how precious their lives are to Him.

Foster care is always a roller-coaster ride, and this case was no different. With each day, each month, and each mound of paperwork submitted, Ryan and I faithfully served the boys and prayed for their future. Just like with Stormy, the boys' story is not mine to tell, but we found ourselves, again, in discussions of our intentions for adoption. Though this choice was a bit harder than our decision to adopt Stormy, God made it clear to us that moving forward with adoption was the plan He had in mind.

Five hundred and six days after meeting the boys, we loaded up our two vans (we never did get around to purchasing a bigger van; instead, we now have a fleet of vehicles) and headed to the courthouse for a second time. On October 13, 2021, Coleman and Christian Hensley joined our family . . . and officially completed our foster care and adoption journey.

Walking through foster care and three adoptions in two years was not something I had pinned on my life's vision board. Neither was having a disabled child. My hopes and dreams revolved around being self-reliant and safe. Yet God had in mind a wild, reckless plan full of love that was much better than anything I could've thought up. This road has been paved with challenges, for sure. No day is easy. Most days are exhausting and overwhelming, filled with countless uncertainties about the future. The same can be said of life before trusting fully in God's plan.

Life without Christ is exhausting and overwhelming, and the future is uncertain. No matter how scrappy you are and how much fight and grit you have, you cannot control your circumstances. Freedom is found in letting go.

When I let loose of the reins and leaned in fully to trust God and His good plans, I freed myself up from having to try to keep it all together. I accepted that even in the most difficult moments of life, His hope keeps me content. When I'm sitting in a surgical waiting room, when I'm having another fight with my tween, when I'm exhausted from chasing two toddlers around all day, when I miss being able to finish one conversation with my husband interruption free—there is hope in the eternal.

There's a saying in the foster and adoption world coined by Jamie Finn: "Every word I speak, every dish I scrub, every diaper

I change, every spill I clean that's done out of love for my Savior is divinely transformed from a mother's chore to a daughter's worship." Tackling life's challenges as a form of worship to our Creator allows us to transform the mundane into something beautiful.

Your worship might be serving as the primary caregiver for an elderly parent, or restocking the freezer section overnight at the local grocery store, or teaching a classroom full of rambunctious preschoolers. Whatever your act of worship is, "work heartily, as for the Lord and not for men, knowing that from the Lord you will receive the inheritance as your reward. You are serving the Lord Christ" (Colossians 3:23–24). My prayer for you (and me) is that the things of earth will continue to grow strangely dim to us as we keep our focus heavenward and on our beautiful, eternal inheritance.

A full courtroom for Stormy's adoption on National Adoption Day,
November 23, 2019, in Dallas, Texas

The Hensley Eight are officially formed when Coleman and Christian are adopted on October 13, 2021, in McKinney, Texas

CHAPTER THIRTEEN

When Restoration Comes

We rejoice in hope of the glory of God.

ROMANS 5:2

id you know there's only *one* book in the sixty-six books that make up the Bible that offers a blessing to the person who reads the entire book? It's almost as if John, the author of Revelation, knew he would be writing about some heavy stuff, so he included a free "gift with purchase" to entice the reader to stick it out. Revelation 1:3 says, "Blessed is the one who reads aloud the words of this prophecy, and blessed are those who hear, and who keep what is written in it, for the time is near."

Many Christians stay away from the book of Revelation for a variety of reasons. It feels confusing. It can seem scary. It may be difficult to decipher between allegory or imagery and the literal events yet to take place. Some people just never make it that far in their Bible reading plan. I've found myself in all of these situations at various seasons of my life.

Until 2007, I hadn't really consulted the Scriptures beyond searching for a set of rules I assumed I needed to be following, a cute Scripture that would work well on a T-shirt, or a reference on Sunday mornings. My outlook on the Bible changed when I was faced with the reality of a child with a lifelong disability who would never walk, never eat by mouth, possibly never speak, and would depend on me to constantly advocate for his well-being. This resulted in the loss of my career, the loss of my dream of a healthy family, and the loss of the ease of life I had flippantly taken for granted. So many losses piled on me at once, leaving me broken, empty, and yearning for a source of hope to help me move forward in what was clearly God's plan for my life and my family.

When life shatters, we Christians face a fork in the road of our spiritual walk. We must decide: Do we lean into the Scriptures and try to understand God for who He is? Or do we walk away from the faith, if only for a season? Where do we put our hope when our circumstances abruptly change—when life gets difficult and we don't have the energy to continue? God's Word says He has plans to give us "a future and a hope" (Jeremiah 29:11), but what exactly is hope?

Hope isn't just a feeling of expectation or yearning for a desired outcome. It is having a deep-rooted sense of trust. When we "place our trust" in Christ, we are saying our faith is in Jesus, the Son of God, who was crucified for our sins, raised from the grave three days after death, and is now residing in heaven with the Father and preparing a place for us. We know there will come a time when He will return for us, His church. Because of God's love, this gospel, the good news, is available to us.

What is it exactly we're being invited to be a part of when we accept the gospel?

As a mom of six, I get enough birthday invitations from my kids' classmates to keep our social calendar full at all times. Do we attend every birthday party we're invited to? Of course not. But the important information on each invitation is always the same: who, what, when, where, and why . . . and please RSVP. Let's consider the gospel presentation as an invitation to heaven.

Who: *Everyone* is offered a chance to spend eternity in heaven. To those who have accepted Christ and the free gift of the gospel, their names are written on the guest list, the Lamb's book of life (Revelation 21:27). The names on that list have RSVPed *yes* and will be in attendance for eternity.

What: Heaven will be a feast and a celebration, but it will also be the restoration of all that was broken when sin entered the world. In heaven there will be no pain, no crying, and no death. Our bodies will be restored and no illness will affect us again. More than that, our relationship with God will not be hindered in any way, and we will have direct access to the Father in person and for all time (Revelation 21:3–4).

When: Upon completion of your time on earth, if you've accepted Christ, your next and final destination will be heaven. The Word says to be absent from the body is to be present with the Lord (2 Corinthians 5:8). Christ will return to earth, as He promised us in John 14:3, and we, His followers, eagerly anticipate that glorious event. Each passing day brings us one day closer to Christ's return for His church.

Where: Our destination is heaven. Look for the crystal sea (Revelation 4:6), the rainbow encircling the throne (Revelation 4:3), the gates made of pearls, and the streets of gold (Revelation 21:21).

Why: The ultimate goal is to be united with our Father, communing freely without barriers. Heaven will restore Eden. We will spend eternity in fellowship with God, worshiping Him, working passionately, and enjoying the beautiful surroundings of heaven without a temptation to sin. In his final book in the Chronicles of Narnia series, C. S. Lewis wrote, "All their life in this world and all their adventures in Narnia had only been the cover and the title page: now at last they were beginning Chapter One of the Great Story which no one on earth has read: which goes on forever: in which every chapter is better than the one before."[19]

There are numerous misconceptions about heaven, which are often rooted in a misunderstanding of Scripture or viewing death without a biblical worldview. Let me make it clear that going to heaven will not make you someone's guardian angel. Our bodies will not transform from human being to angelic being upon death. Besides, heaven doesn't need more angels. God created His angel army, and to insinuate He was a few short is unbiblical.

I believe that when we enter heaven, we will be so mesmerized by seeing the face of Jesus that we will have no interest in even thinking back to our times on this broken earth and watching over our loved ones. The earthly constraint of time doesn't exist in heaven, so during a heavenly blink of our eyes, one hundred years on earth could have passed.

I challenge you to consider the ideas and assumptions you hold about heaven and run them through the test of Scripture to see if you can confirm or deny your speculations.

May our eyes be opened to the truth of God's Word and His promises of heaven.

Learning about the logistics of heaven changes the way we operate in our daily lives. Understanding eternity affects how we navigate the temporal.

Pastor Francis Chan illustrates this concept using a long rope, about twenty feet in length, with two inches of the end painted red.[20] The red portion, which looks ridiculously tiny when compared to the enormous remaining part of the rope, represents our seventy, eighty, or ninety years of life on this planet, if we're lucky. The lengthy unpainted portion of the rope represents billions and billions of years of eternity. This lifetime is a vapor of mist, a flash in the pan, a blip on the radar in comparison to all of eternity. Yet many of us focus on our temporal happiness in the here and now rather than making decisions in light of the infinite amount of time we will spend in our eternal destination.

Southern gospel music played a key role in my upbringing. With four-part vocal arrangements and call-back lyrics, it typically focuses on heaven and on enduring earthly trials until Christ's return. From my early years this music directed me to look forward to peace in the valley.

Yet until Hayden's life, I didn't have the context to fully grasp the beauty that future restoration holds. Knowing now that my son's earthly, mangled body will one day be restored, upright, and movable makes the hope of heaven more real than any lyrical verse I've casually sung since the day I was big enough to hold a Baptist hymnal. My perspective on every word I sing is different now than it was before.

When I hear songs stating how every knee will bow, what I hear is that Hayden's legs will be able to move appropriately one day because he too will bow. When I sing of the clouds being rolled back upon Christ's second coming, I'm reassured that God has not forgotten us, but He will return to make all things right one day. When hymns encourage us to turn our eyes toward Jesus, I wonder what makes us turn our eyes toward Him.

Jesus told His followers to store up for themselves "treasures in heaven, where neither moth nor rust destroys and where thieves do not break in and steal" (Matthew 6:20). When we view life with our eyes set on heaven, the eternal treasures we store up are different from those stored only on this earth.

I don't get too worked up over living in a certain neighborhood or having the right zip code, but heaven will be the ultimate neighborhood to live in. Of course the housing will be top-notch, but I'm most excited about who will be there. God Himself will be present with His children! There won't be a temple because His dwelling place will be with His kids (Revelation 21:22).

Randy Alcorn says, "For the believer, earth is the most hell they will ever experience; but for the lost person, earth is the most heaven they will ever experience."[21] If we're chasing earthly treasures that will one day be rusted, destroyed, and burned, what a sad, dire situation to find ourselves in.

The blessing of my son's challenging life is that it has taught me more than any healthy, typical life ever could have. Difficult circumstances have gifted me the bravery to walk faithfully into spaces I would never have considered, such as foster care and adoption. I've learned to look at life's circumstances through an eternal lens. Trivial things are just that to me—trivial. Things that bother most people simply don't matter to me. In my world, each day can turn from life to death in an instant. I've saved my son's life more times than I can count, and after living that reality, things like how clean your house is, the make and model of your car, or how many figures your annual income has are not worth my consideration. I was not called to this earth for such things.

When I do feel myself getting worked up over something, I often ask myself, *Does this have eternal value? Will this issue or conflict matter in eternity?* If the answer is no, I bless and release it. We have been put here on a mission, and we cannot lose focus and give in to distractions.

Sufferers often sing the loudest about the joy to come. Yet we're not only encouraged by the treasures we will have in heaven. God ordained whatever you're going through right now. He isn't throwing this thing together at the last minute. He had a divine plan before the creation of the world. He's not caught off guard or surprised by anything. We may not understand His ways, but He is a God who can be trusted.

During His thirty-three years on planet earth, Jesus performed many miracles. He did this for several reasons. One was to reveal to us the kingdom that is to come. When He healed the leper, the lame, the blind, and the bleeding, Jesus demonstrated to the world that the kingdom of God is the cure for illness and disease. When He raised a dead girl back to life—and later overcame His own death on a cross— He made known that death is not welcome in God's kingdom. When He turned water into wine in His first recorded miracle—and later, on two occasions, fed thousands with just a few loaves and fish— He reminded us that heaven will be a wedding feast celebration for Christ, the groom, and His bride, the church. During His time on earth, Jesus declared the kingdom to come and made known that in eternity, all things will be set right.

Unfortunately, in this broken world full of pain, some things will never be restored. My son will never walk. He will never have a straight spine. He will never feel the need to use the restroom and take care of such a simple bodily function that three-year-olds do. He will never hop in his car and drive to a friend's house to grab pizza, play video games, and discuss who to ask to the homecoming dance. And that is painful. It isn't fair. But when my God, who is so faithful, has given me such beauty and hope, I refuse to wallow in the temporal pain I've been assigned to bear. I will set my eyes on eternity and the joy that is to come.

With every fiber of my being, I trust and believe my good, good Father and His plans. Through God's grace, mine is not a hopeless reality. It's the exact opposite, in fact. Because of the promise God has made to us, I can put all my hope in Him. I know without a shadow of a doubt that my son will walk one day. His first steps will be into the arms of Jesus. His first meal will be at the wedding feast of the Lamb. One day, Hayden will speak clearly. His voice will not falter when he sings his songs of praise in heaven. My son will not need a ventilator to keep him alive when he sleeps. In heaven, there is no night.

And I will find my rest when everything about this life comes to fruition. We live our lives on this planet as one pixel of an enormous painting that we cannot see. We stare at our own tiny pixel and dwell there. But in heaven, we will step back and see the full, beautiful tapestry God has been creating, in which we each have the privilege to play a role.

Every tear I have shed will be wiped from my face by my Father. I will spend eternity learning all the ways God used our family and our story to touch people I never met or spoke to. I'll find out about each bystander who ever watched my rainbow family wheel and walk out of our clown-car van and wondered, *How are they still smiling and full of joy? What's giving them the strength?* I'll see how God's hand moved His paintbrush across the canvas.

I am thankful to be considered worthy of being a part of something so beautiful. On that day, this life of suffering will all be validated, and any crowns or treasures I've earned I will lay back at His feet.

CHAPTER FOURTEEN

Family Ties

You do for family!

—FRANKIE HECK

As we believers anticipate eternity, we attempt to live all of our earthly moments to the fullest. But even while living for the kingdom, mundane tasks still exist. With six kids, there's really nothing calm or boring going on in our home. A normal day for us is as wild and chaotic as you can imagine. As the matriarch of chaos, I wear many hats, usually at the same time. No two days look exactly the same for us.

To satisfy any curiosity you may have, I'll share a "Day in the Life" here.

A Typical Wednesday

5:10 a.m.	My alarm goes off, I read and do some of my Bible study homework before the twins wake up . . . because once they're up, all bets are off. Ryan makes coffee and brings it to me every morning of my life. #blessed!
5:45 a.m.	Twins are up, fighting over who Mom holds first and demanding a sippy cup filled with apple juice and a 'nack (snack).
6:05 a.m.	School-age kids wake up and begin making their lunches, getting breakfast and vitamins, and getting dressed. (All clothes get laid out the night before and the breakfast menu is selected as well. We do as much planning ahead as possible to make the morning go smoothly.)
7:00 a.m.	One parent drives three of the kids to school in the next town over, while the other parent gets the twins dressed and waits for the nurse of the day to arrive, who will then wake Hayden and begin his morning treatment routine.
9:00 a.m.	A family friend comes to watch the twins and help with household chores while I begin homeschool lessons with Hayden (two days a week).
11:30 a.m.	Morning homeschool time concludes and midday treatments with the nurse begin for Hayden. I prepare lunch for the twins while they play.
12:00 noon	I serve lunch to the twins and their nap time begins immediately after. Caregiver leaves.
12:30 p.m.	While the twins sleep, we kick off Hayden's homeschool afternoon session.
2:00 p.m.	The twins wake up and homeschool closes down. I attempt to prepare a quick and easy meal for dinner.
3:00 p.m.	Hayden's therapist of the day arrives for a treatment session.
3:45 p.m.	I load the twins in the van and head to school to pick up the other kids from football practice, honor choir, and after-school care.
5:00 p.m.	Everyone is home together for a quick meal before Wednesday night church activities begin.
5:45 p.m.	The teen and school-age kids leave for church services with a nurse, who accompanies Hayden to youth group.
7:45 p.m.	One parent gets the twins bathed and settled into bed while the other parent drives to church to do evening pickup.
8:15 p.m.	Everyone is home and showering, finishing homework and chores, and laying out clothes for the next day. Nurse begins night treatments with Hayden.
9:00 p.m.	Lights out for all. We are tired! But we made it . . . and will do it all again tomorrow.

Each commitment we keep on our busy schedule and every interaction I have with my kids and my husband is an opportunity for me to model my trust in God's goodness and sovereignty. I fail plenty, but thankfully, God's grace is big enough to cover my shortcomings.

In a loud, chaotic house, I'm often overstimulated, and I confess I don't operate well from a place of overstimulation. If that resonates with you, never underestimate the value of a good weighted blanket and a set of noise-canceling headphones. I need moments to recharge and regulate myself before I can offer any help to a family member who is dysregulated and struggling. In those moments, I thank God for the peace only He can offer and remind myself that there will be peace for me one day.

∽

WHERE ARE THEY NOW?

As my story comes to a close, I want to offer a status update on some of the people I've introduced you to. Hayden is fifteen now, and his health is stable, averaging one or two surprise hospital stays a year. He is my only homeschooled student now, and you'd think we could accomplish incredible amounts of schooling daily, but keeping a strict therapy and treatment schedule (with twin toddlers underfoot) tends to hinder our productivity, as I'm sure you can imagine.

I don't know what the future holds for Hayden. Sometimes people ask me how long he will live. I usually respond, "I don't know—how long will *you* live?" Truthfully, we never anticipated being given this many years with Hayden, and we're thankful for each of them. As he approaches adulthood, we are setting our eyes on the dream of building a custom home to provide Hayden with an apartment-style living arrangement. We hope to foster as much independence as possible while also having easy access to him so we can serve as his nurses when he ages out of his current benefits.

Ryan and I intend to fully enjoy our empty nesting years with a *plus one*, and that will be just fine. We've endured each day one at a time, and that's how we'll continue to live our lives until God calls us (or Hayden) home.

Grayson is twelve now and has a kind, tender, and spicy temperament. He's lived a unique life as a second-born firstborn. Though he has a big brother, it was Grayson who walked first, who talked first, and who carries a heavy load to lead by example for his younger siblings. He is a thinker who trusts God and His ultimate plan, and it encourages me to see such faith in a young man. Stubborn and strong in convictions, this one will move mountains one day. He is in middle school at a private Christian school, and we're actively searching for the balance of counseling and disciplining a tween amid the noise and chaos of two toddlers and three other kids.

Grayson's life brings moments of mourning to my mama heart. Simple things remind me of all that Hayden has lost in this life. Grayson doesn't have a cell phone yet. On the night of the middle school homecoming dance, he went to dinner with friends before meeting us at the football game. Hayden was grounded from his cell phone that night, so we let Grayson take it in case he needed to reach us. Sitting in the football stands, surrounded by people, a wave of grief washed over me when I received a text from my saved contact #HPtheVIP that read, "We just left the restaurant, heading to the game." For a millisecond in time, I thought Hayden was reporting that to me. Then I remembered, and I mourned that Hayden couldn't be dropped off at a restaurant alone. He doesn't have a group of friends or even the ability to eat food by mouth. Hayden wouldn't just hop into a standard vehicle and be driven to the game. I grieved all of those things in the span of a split second, while sitting in a crowd of football fans. And I will continue to do so for as long as I'm here on this planet.

Holding space in the tension between being happy for your healthy child and sad for your sick one is a heavy calling. Grayson's first time driving, his first day of college, his wedding—all these things will bring a tinge of sadness with them, alongside the happiness. I cope by recognizing my emotions and bringing them to the Lord. God the Father knows well the intricacies of sadness a parent often bears.

Ethan is enjoying fourth grade at the same school his big brother and younger sister attend. He was born with an easy, lovable spirit, and he's a treat to spend time with. He sees the beauty in life and finds joy in nearly all circumstances. When Stormy joined our family, Ethan made the jump from youngest child to big brother like a champ. The two of them have their rifts and frustrations with each other, as all siblings do. Personalities collide in a family of eight. Ryan and I pray for the day when all of our kids will discover the ease of being friends.

In a family this large, certain dynamics jive easier than others, and I love watching the special bond Ethan and Hayden have. These boys enjoy spending time together and even schedule times to binge-watch their favorite show. Knowing Hayden has a built-in bestie in Ethan is precious to me.

Stormy has just started kindergarten and is excited to be going to school with two of her big brothers. She's a pleasant student, eager to read and learn. She's a wonderful big sister to her little brothers and is working diligently to become a great little sister to her older brothers.

When the twins arrived in our home as emergency foster placements, Stormy had just turned three and had been in our home for one year. She transitioned from being the youngest child, being doted on and treated like a princess, to being asked to grow up overnight. Two years after their arrival, we're still working out attachment issues.

Adopting from foster care hasn't been easy. But just because something is difficult doesn't mean we shouldn't do it. Every member of our family has been in counseling at some point in their life, and right now it's my and Stormy's turn. There is no shame in seeking resources and assistance from professionals. I trusted God's plan when He brought Stormy into our lives, and even in the challenging moments, I continue to trust God's sovereign plan.

I have wanted twins ever since I was a child. Each of my grandmothers delivered twins, so I have two sets of twin aunts and uncles. I thought for sure the old wives' tale would come true, that it would skip a generation and I would have twins. But that wasn't the case for me, so I gave up my dream. Who knew it would actually happen through a surprise road trip phone call? And obviously a lot of God orchestrating a beautiful plan.

Coleman is two and a half and the older twin by sixty seconds. He is a replica of Stormy; their facial features and body builds are remarkably similar. When he arrived in our home at six days old, looking just like his sister, it was as if God was gifting to us the years we missed out on from Stormy's early life. We no longer had to wonder what she looked like as an infant. Coleman has a sweet, calm temperament, though he can be feisty, as most two-year-olds can be. He enjoys reading books and treasures time to play quietly alone, a rare commodity in a house full of eight loud humans.

Christian, despite being born the larger twin by a full pound, is now a tiny two-year-old filled to the max with the perfect combination of spice and sweetness. Born with a handful of minor health issues (most things feel minor compared to Hayden's menagerie of diagnoses), Christian has been brave and resilient and is currently healthy and stable.

The gift of multiples is that any exposure to unwelcomed substances in utero is cut to half strength, hopefully keeping both safer and preserving their health more than a singleton birth. Even in the womb, the boys were looking after each other in that unique twin way.

Ryan and I have enjoyed the past eighteen years of our marriage and have already lived more adventures than I could have ever anticipated that cold January afternoon when we vowed to embark on whatever God had for us. We are teammates, and on this battlefield of parenting, there's not much time to hold grudges. If you stay mad at each other for too long, especially over minor stuff, the whole operation will crash and burn. We've learned about grace and forgiveness and how to be a team player. Most important, we've had countless lessons on how to die to self. I feel honored that God chose me to be Ryan's partner for life, tackling all these holy assignments together, side by side.

In terms of our foster and adoption journey, our home is now officially closed. We are at capacity with six children eighteen and under. This is no longer a yes we are called to walk in, so we have accepted the no. However, our passionate desire to serve the vulnerable isn't closed. We find other ways to support foster families and our former agency, Buckner International. My prayer is that our family will encourage others and that the fire of our passion will light many torches to join in the mission of foster and adoptive care.

If God has prompted your heart in this direction, lean into it. Trust Him and believe His good plans. Lock your eyes on eternity and then move your feet—walk in a yes until it's a no. Be brave. Say yes. Make a phone call to an agency. Send an email to a ministry. Stop thinking and dreaming. Start doing.

❦

Today, as you step out into the world, I pray God will give you a fresh lens to view the world around you. May you see the temporal world for what it is—temporary. I encourage you to bravely live your life with your heart and mind set on eternity, never wavering in your knowledge and trust of who God is. From a place of security and faith, may you make decisions that set you apart from the world.

Find the ministry, the call, the area of interest that will make an impact for the kingdom, and run full steam ahead into serving in that space. Then tell your story. Share it with the world and encourage those around you to do the same. May we all live passionate lives of purpose and say yes to God's call with full confidence, no matter how reckless we may appear to those around us, always keeping our hope in Him.

The Hensley Eight, ready and excited to say YES to the next adventure
God has in store, Prosper, Texas, 2022

APPENDIX

Helpful Strategies

*P*erhaps your family isn't built around a disability or foster care, but you have a challenging set of circumstances that don't fit the mold of the world around you. You might find yourself in need of support and encouragement for a variety of reasons. Even if your family is as put together as the Cleavers, we all face struggles at some time in this life. As the old adage goes, you're either coming out of a trial, you're in the middle of a trial, or you're about to walk into a trial. Here are some reminders for when you find yourself in need of a helping hand and encouragement.

ACCEPT HELP

For many years, I was too prideful to accept much help from those who offered. Feeling like I had something to prove, I declined assistance from friends trying to ease my load. I wouldn't let people get too close because they might see my dirty house and figure out that I didn't have it all together. Let them see it! If someone is trying to support you and show up for you (literally), then move out of your own way and let them!

When we pridefully attempt to do everything on our own, we remove the opportunity for the church to operate as a body. Scripture tells us we all play a role in serving, and by not accepting help, it could be that you're not letting a brother or sister utilize their gifting. Plus, don't you feel great when you've helped someone? You're blessed by helping. Don't intentionally block someone's blessing in an attempt to be perceived as strong.

SET YOUR CIRCLE

Planning ahead is always helpful, especially when it comes to finding your community. In my family's case, we often find ourselves in situations where we need aid and assistance. Our extended family came with us into this unique life of disabilities and adoptions. But the friendships we've made took time and investment to grow and develop.

Church circles sometimes use Christianese words and phrases, such as "doing life with" or "community" or "small group," to explain the concept of being in close proximity and relationship to friends and fellow believers who will speak into your life. It's important to find people to be a part of your community for all the good days (the birthday parties, cookouts, holiday celebrations, etc.). But it's especially vital for the bad days (a job loss, when your child is in the hospital, the death of a loved one). Decide now who you would call on the worst day of your life. Think that through ahead of time, before life's drama takes you to the point of desperate need and you're left scrambling.

I've heard it said that when lying on your deathbed, there's only room for eight people to stand around you. Who will those eight people be for you? If you don't have that handful of people in mind, you may need to spend some time investing in deep, meaningful relationships. That's not always easy if you have a child who is a challenge, or you have multiple children, or your spouse travels or works inconvenient hours. There are a million reasons to set building friendships on the back burner. Let me encourage you today to start getting serious about setting your circle.

But don't only think of who you would call in a tragedy; aim to be the type of friend *someone else* would call on their worst day. We can't just be consumers of friends and receivers of help. We also need to provide support for others, without expecting anything in return. We want to be the hands and feet of Jesus, and showing up for our friends is one of the ways we live out our faith.

HOW TO HELP FAMILIES IN NEED OF EXTRA TLC

So you've committed to being a good friend with pure motives who looks like Jesus to those around you. What's the next practical step to take? Oftentimes, we want to help others but have no idea where to begin, and instead may freeze up and do nothing. Here are some ways you can start helping those around you today.

PRAY

This seems so basic, easy, and simple that it usually gets forgotten. We holler a flippant, "I'm praying for you" to a friend who is struggling, then we never do it. Commit to actually praying for your friend—behind her back *and* to her face.

A couple of years ago, a dear friend of mine was struggling with multiple health and family issues, so I decided to journal a daily prayer in a cheap spiral notebook. During the month of January, I jotted down my conversations with God about my friend, lifting up her health concerns and also praying for her tender heart. After collecting thirty-one handwritten prayers, one for each day, I delivered the notebook to her. It was such a joy for me to see her receive these simple prayers when I approached the throne on her behalf. She felt loved and honored knowing I had been praying for her, and writing them in the notebook helped me hold myself accountable for praying for her.

This is a great way to support a loved one who isn't local to you. A prayer journal, or even a card with a single written prayer, can be easily mailed across the country or around the world.

FOOD

We all have to eat, right? Any family with special needs knows that at any moment, a lengthy hospital stay could be just around the corner. Living with a chronically ill person means living in constant anticipation of the other shoe falling. When a hospital admission happens in our family, we still have five other mouths to feed at home, and they're going to be hungry whether Mom and Dad are at home or in the ICU.

When a family receives an emergency foster placement, the last thing the parents think about is meal prep. They're trying to get to know the new human who's living with them, who only hours before they didn't know existed.

For any family who's experiencing a big adjustment or is dealing with extreme stress, bringing them food will be a tremendous blessing! Don't get wrapped around the axle here thinking you have to provide them with something homemade from your special secret recipe. There is a reason Chick-fil-A makes trays of nuggets and puts iced tea in a gallon! Go buy a fully cooked rotisserie chicken, a bag of salad, and a box of cookies. Families in a bind aren't longing to try homemade sourdough bread from your grandmother's 1921 starter—they just want to be fed!

If you know of a family who will be needing meals for a while, set up a Meal Train website and share it with others. Pro tip: instead of scheduling a meal to be brought each day, have people sign up for every other day. There will probably be leftovers from each meal, and you don't want to bombard the family with more food than they can eat.

Also, don't ask a family if they need a meal. Tell them you're bringing food and let them pick the time and alert you of any allergies. (If you bring something and find out they already have a meal for that day, they can freeze it and save it for later.)

Families sometimes say they don't need anything, but I promise you they do. They just don't want to be a burden. Go ahead and take the decision-making off the plate of a family already in a stressful situation by declaring how you will be serving them and limiting the questions they have to answer.

Many hospitals offer meal cards. If you know someone with a family member in the hospital, you could purchase meal cards for them. Or you can give them a DoorDash or Uber Eats gift card. Being tied to the bedside of a hospital patient makes grabbing food difficult, so having food delivered is helpful.

LAUNDRY

One of the biggest blessings of my life, especially as a mom of six children, is when a friend shows up to my (usually messy) house, sees laundry baskets everywhere, and just starts folding laundry. All praise and honor and glory to God! More than anything, your friend will thank you for this simple task.

When our twins were a few weeks old, a friend texted, "I'm coming over with coffee and a box of diapers. Be there in five." She came in, set down her deliveries, and started washing dishes in my overflowing sink. I've never felt more loved. Hallelujah and amen! Doing those small, simple tasks is more helpful than you might imagine. Especially to the family that is overwhelmed by even the basic things.

Some laundry services will pick up dirty clothes, wash them, and return them to your home. If that is available in your area, you and a few friends or church members could purchase a gift card for laundry services and give it to a foster family or to a family whose child is in the hospital.

YARD WORK

Tedious must-do tasks are the last thing on the mind of a person going through a difficult time. Offer to mow the yard of a newly widowed neighbor, a woman whose husband is deployed, or any family experiencing a stressful time. Send your teenage son over to mow and pull weeds, or ask your life group to gather funds and hire someone to stop by weekly and take care of the yard.

You could use this same strategy to hire a cleaning lady to come in and tidy up while the family is adjusting to new family members or spending time at the hospital. (Check with their comfort level first to see if they would consider this a practical gift.)

DIAPERS AND HAND-ME-DOWNS

For foster families who take emergency placements of babies, there are never enough diapers. Ask the parents what size the child is in, then Instacart or drop off a box or two of diapers and wipes. Find out what size clothes and shoes the child wears and see if your own kids have any hand-me-downs you could pass along. Or toys they no longer play with. They don't have to be fancy or brand new. Families will appreciate your thoughtfulness of showing up with useful resources.

SEE THE SIBLINGS

Oftentimes siblings feel forgotten when Mom and Dad are at the hospital with a sick child or taking in a new foster placement. An offer to provide pickup and drop-off help for sports practices and games, tutoring, school, and other normal activities could alleviate a huge amount of stress on the parents. Or invite the sibling to dinner or a movie to give them something fun to look forward to in the midst of chaos.

BRING TISSUES

Sometimes your friend just needs a shoulder to cry on. Offer a listening ear and a zipped lip. Don't try to solve all the problems or find a way to look on the bright side of a crummy situation. Your role as a supportive friend might just be sitting in the sadness when tragedy strikes—after the husband walks out, the teenage daughter reveals her pregnancy, or the cancer diagnosis is confirmed. The closeness of a friend who is not afraid to show up in a difficult, sad, or scary circumstance is a true gift.

Epilogue

I started this book by stating that God is real and has a plan. And the Enemy wants to thwart God's plan. Writing this book has been one of the most difficult things I've ever done, and it required a daily fight on the spiritual battlefield. During my months of writing, Hayden had an emergency brain surgery, I was down with four different illnesses, our family had to move out of our home for three weeks for an HGTV show episode we filmed, we endured the challenging transitions of sending two of our children to kindergarten and middle school, our twins both had surgery, one of our kids started counseling . . . the list goes on. Yet here I am. And you hold this book in your hands today.

This project sat in my head as a dream for years. My prayer has always been that at least one life would be changed by a reader coming to know Christ more fully. I hope this book changed you to some degree and that its message will stay with you. It has been my life's privilege to share my story, my hope, and my God with you.

Acknowledgments

If I had written this book when the dream to do so first entered my heart nine years ago, the story would not have been complete. I had lots of life to live before my story would be ready to share with you. And turning my experiences and life lessons into this book would not have been possible without help from others.

First off, this book would not exist without the encouragement and support of my husband. Ryan, you have supported every wild dream I ever thought up, no questions asked. Thank you for all the hours you watched the kids so I could sneak away to write. I'm blessed to live this life with you by my side.

To my kids: Hayden, Grayson, Ethan, Stormy, Coleman, and Christian—thank you for your incredible patience over this last year while I was writing. You always encouraged me and remained excited for me and the entire process while the book was being created. I hope I've made you proud, and I look forward to you sharing our family's story with your own families one day.

Thank you to the Remnant for throwing oars, night or day, and being my loudest cheerleaders. God gifted me beyond my wildest dreams when he brought you two into my life. May our friendship last into eternity, long after our matching bracelets have rusted and tarnished.

To Bob Goff, the Dream Big Team, and Onsite Workshops—this book would never have made it out of my head and onto paper without your tender care and love, along with the healing you brought to me in the hills of Tennessee in 2018. Thank you for clearing pathways and helping me find my voice.

Thank you to Tara-Leigh Cobble, The Bible Recap, and D-Group for changing my life more than any Bible study or reading plan ever has. God certainly moved in mighty ways through your faithful obedience and your gift of making Scripture come to life. I've never had so much fun learning Scripture and living beyond myself.

To Jana Schmitt, thank you for the countless hours of collaborating with me to process heavy burdens. Our years together healed wounds I thought were permanent. You could see me when I couldn't even recognize myself. Thank you for being one of my biggest encouragers and always believing in me and my dreams.

Finally, to our family's prayer warriors, especially Aunt Gail—you have bruised knees and tear-stained cheeks, and my family is here today as living proof that God heard your prayers. Thank you for standing in the gap for us, interceding on our behalf when life was too hard and too exhausting and we were too broken to pray. Your prayers sustained us on the days we weren't sure we would survive. We are forever grateful to you.

About the Author

JOHNNA (pronounced *John-NUH*) is a Christ follower, author, blogger, and all-time coordinator of chaos. She is passionate about sharing the eternal hope she found in Jesus after her firstborn son was diagnosed with spina bifida, a neural tube defect, in 2007. That diagnosis turned her entire life upside down. After a seven-month-long NICU hospital stay, her son finally came home, and he has been making waves ever since.

In the moments when all her hopes and dreams for her family fell apart, she came to realize with certainty that this world is not our final destination. Johnna learned valuable lessons about the sanctity of all life, no matter the diagnosis or disability, and her hope in heaven is even more secure as she looks forward to the restoration eternity will bring for her son.

Johnna navigates her life with an eternal perspective and lives bravely in this temporal world by choosing to say yes when God calls her to an adventure. Some of those adventures have included building a full house and family of eight through childbirth and adoption. Many of her decisions may seem reckless to the world, but knowing her home is in heaven, Johnna is not afraid to look a little crazy. Johnna is called to encourage people to stop living timid lives of distraction and to bravely say yes to what God calls them to.

As an authentic truth teller, Johnna points people to Jesus in the middle of her own chaos through her blog and her books. With six children of several ages and stages, of various races and abilities, her family is a wild, rowdy bunch that keeps her busy. Johnna and her energetic husband, Ryan, have been married for eighteen years and enjoy being on mission together in their passion to be pro-life, from womb to tomb.

In her sacred free time, Johnna can be spotted on the patio of a Tex-Mex restaurant, elbow deep in chips and salsa, talking with close friends about her kids, her love for Texas, the Bible, and the occasional conspiracy theory. Otherwise, she's introverting at home, journaling under her weighted blanket while wearing noise-canceling headphones with a cup of hot coffee in hand.

To stay up to date with Johnna's adventures, visit her website, JohnnaHensley.com.

Endnotes

CHAPTER 2

1   Google Dictionary, s.v. "outlier."

CHAPTER 4

2   Dr. Seuss, *Horton Hears a Who!* (New York: Random House Books, 1954).
3   Centers for Disease Control and Prevention, "Data & Statistics on Spina Bifida," https://www.cdc.gov/ncbddd/spinabifida/data.html.
4   Spina Bifida Association, "New & Expectant Parents," https://www.spinabifidaassociation.org/expectant-parents/.

CHAPTER 7

5   *Merriam-Webster Dictionary*, s.v. "grief," https://www.merriam-webster.com/dictionary/grief.

CHAPTER 8

6   Pyramid Educational Consultants, Picture Exchange
     Communication System (PECS)®, Developed by Andy Bondy, PhD
     & Lori Frost, MS, CCC-SLP, https://pecsusa.com/pecs/.
7   The Bradley Method, https://www.bradleybirth.com.

CHAPTER 9

8   Bethania Palma, "No, Darth Vader Didn't Actually Say 'Luke, I Am
     Your Father,'" Snopes, July 20, 2022, https://www.snopes.com/fact-
     check/star-wars-luke-i-am-your-father/.
9   "Christians Don't Read Their Bible," Ponce Foundation, http://
     poncefoundation.com/christians-dont-read-their-bible/.
10   Aaron Earls, "More Americans Read the Bible During the
     Pandemic," Lifeway Research, October 21, 2021, https://research.
     lifeway.com/2021/10/21/more-americans-read-the-bible-during-
     the-pandemic/#:~:text=A%202016%20Lifeway%20Research%20
     study,a%20few%20sentences%20or%20less.
11   Google Dictionary, s.v. "evangelical."
12   Tony Evans, *Tony Evans Bible Commentary* (Nashville, TN: Holman
     Bible Publishers, 2019), 1083.
13   "The Forbidden Chapter: Isaiah 53 in the Hebrew Bible," Tree of Life
     Ministries, YouTube, https://www.youtube.com/watch?v=cGz9BVJ_
     k6s.
14   For more information on The Bible Recap Bible reading plan, visit
     http://www.thebiblerecap.com.

CHAPTER 11

15   "Information on Fruitless Pear Trees," SF Gate, September 10,
     2020, https://homeguides.sfgate.com/information-fruitless-pear-
     trees-38748.html.
16   Tony Evans, *Tony Evans Bible Commentary* (Nashville, TN: Holman
     Bible Publishers, 2019), 1051.
17   "Information on Fruitless Pear Trees," SF Gate, September 10,
     2020, https://homeguides.sfgate.com/information-fruitless-pear-
     trees-38748.html.

CHAPTER 12

18 Charles Spurgeon, https://www.goodreads.com/quotes/1199735-i-have-learned-to-kiss-the-waves-that-throw-me.

CHAPTER 13

19 C. S. Lewis, *The Last Battle* (London: The Bodley Head, 1956), https://www.goodreads.com/quotes/408160-all-their-life-in-this-world-and-all-their-adventures.

20 Francis Chan, "Francis Chan—Rope Illustration (Original)," https://www.youtube.com/watch?v=86dsfBbZfWs.

21 Randy Alcorn, *Heaven* (Wheaton, IL: Tyndale House Publishers, 2004).

ORDER INFORMATION

To order additional copies of this book, please visit
www.redemption-press.com.
Also available at Christian bookstores, Amazon, and Barnes and Noble.

CPSIA information can be obtained
at www.ICGtesting.com
Printed in the USA
BVHW041738270523
664991BV00002B/6